NEW TE...
WIS...
fo...
EVERYONE

NEW
TESTAMENT
WISDOM
for
EVERYONE

TOM
WRIGHT

First published in Great Britain in 2013

Society for Promoting Christian Knowledge
36 Causton Street
London SW1P 4ST
www.spckpublishing.co.uk

Scripture quotations are taken from *The New Testament for Everyone*,
copyright © Nicholas Thomas Wright 2011.

British Library Cataloguing-in-Publication Data
A catalogue record for this book is available from the British Library

ISBN 978–0–281–06937–8
eBook ISBN 978–0–281–06938–5

Typeset by Graphicraft Limited, Hong Kong
First printed in Great Britain by Ashford Colour Press
Subsequently digitally printed in Great Britain

eBook by Graphicraft Limited, Hong Kong

Produced on paper from sustainable forests

For Justin Welby

CONTENTS

INTRODUCTION

I worked for some years as a member of a team of nine. Every month we used to meet for the best part of a day and slog our way through all kinds of issues – big questions of policy, sensitive details about individual people, routine (but important) matters of administration. We were a talkative lot, with strong opinions, a range of different experience and firmly held principles. When I joined the team, the others already possessed an excellent knowledge of the situations and people we would be discussing, and I had to catch up fast. Our conversations were of the rapid-fire type, with argument, wit and sharp insight flashing to and fro.

But there was one member of the team who didn't say as much as the rest. He would sit and listen and ponder. Then, when the rest of us were out of breath, he would often say the one thing we had all overlooked, throwing everything into a new light. The discussion would change course; not necessarily being resolved at once, but continuing at a new level.

That is one of the images I have when I think of 'wisdom'. It doesn't mean knowing all the facts, though having a well-stocked mind is part of it. It doesn't mean being 'clever', thinking up cunning but superficial plans. It doesn't even mean always being right. 'Wisdom' is that strange, elusive quality that draws together knowledge, insight, humility, patience and experience and can then see a situation in many dimensions, like a musician who can hear not only the tune being played but also the different levels of harmony and counterpoint underneath. (Not surprisingly, my quiet but wise colleague is also a musician.)

The Bible is full of wisdom. There are books we think of as 'wisdom literature', notably Proverbs, Ecclesiastes and Job in the Old Testament and, not least, the letter of James in the New. Proverbs turns 'wisdom' into a metaphorical person, a wise lady who invites the young and foolish into her house to learn the wisdom they need. The book as a whole ranges widely: from simple maxims to guide you through life, to deep, rich insights into how to be truly human, to trust and respect our Maker. 'Lady Wisdom' reveals herself as God's assistant, at his right hand, when he made the world. That's picture-language for saying that when God made the world he did so wisely. But it is also an invitation: learn wisdom, and you can be part of God's work in the world here and now.

As well as giving us wisdom *literature*, the Bible gives us wise *characters*. Joseph in the book of Genesis, and Daniel in the book that bears his name, were able, through faith and prayer, to understand dreams and visions that had baffled kings and their counsellors. The great biblical figure of wisdom is King Solomon himself, David's son, who prayed for wisdom to rule God's people, and was given it in abundance. Such people knew that, ultimately, all secrets belong to God, and that sometimes God will make them known to those who ponder and pray – not to bypass ordinary human learning (indeed, Solomon was famous for his encyclopaedic knowledge), but to add an extra, and sometimes vital, dimension.

By the time the 'wisdom' traditions reached Jesus, they had combined three things. First, they prized the solid human knowledge and insight that enable people to see to the heart of a complex issue. Second, they were aware that sometimes what's needed is fresh revelation from the creator God. Third, they knew that 'wisdom' is what the rulers of the world need, and often lack. 'Wisdom' thus combined practical knowledge, fresh God-given revelation, and political application.

We shouldn't be surprised, then, that the earliest Christians saw Jesus himself not only as the greatest ever *teacher* of 'wisdom', but as its greatest living *embodiment*. He drew on a rich range of knowledge about everything from plants to people. He was in himself, they believed, the personal fresh revelation of the living God himself. And he was announcing, and launching, God's kingdom on earth as in heaven. Sometimes he pulled all this together into famous stories, tales of wise and foolish people: the men building houses on rock or on sand, or the girls who were or weren't ready for the wedding party. He told these stories not simply to give general lessons, but to warn his hearers that they needed special wisdom then and there, to see what God was doing and to respond appropriately.

All this explains why, after his death and resurrection, his followers picked up the biblical theme of wisdom and wove it into new patterns around Jesus himself. This little book explores several key moments where we see this happening, and where we are invited to join in and make this wisdom our own. Jesus, these texts tell us, has opened up a whole new world, with God in charge in a new way. It takes all the wisdom we can find, freshly shaped around Jesus' cross and resurrection, to live appropriately within that new world, while the foolish world rumbles on, giving out the same old nonsense and luring people away from the path that leads to life.

That is why, in the passages we explore in this book, we find the same mixture of themes you get in the Old Testament: human stories, fresh revelations, the clash between God's kingdom and the world's, and the challenge to live differently once we understand what's going on. 'O loving wisdom of our God,' says the hymn: that is what we seek, as with ordinary followers of Jesus in every age we come to learn from him, from Wisdom in Person, how to say No to folly and Yes, at every level, to his gracious invitation to life.

Tom Wright

1

THE WISDOM OF THE SPIRIT

GOD'S POWERFUL MYSTERY

1 Corinthians 2.1–5

[1]When I came to you, I didn't come and proclaim God's mystery to you by means of a superior style of speaking or wisdom. [2]No: I decided to know nothing in my dealings with you except Jesus the Messiah, especially his crucifixion. [3]I came to you in weakness, in great fear and trembling. [4]My speech and my proclamation were not in persuasive words of wisdom, but in transparent proof brought home powerfully by the spirit, [5]so that your faith might not be in human wisdom but in God's power.

Life is full of mystery. The deepest, richest and most complex theories that science can ever come up with only serve to highlight the fact that there is still a depth of mystery which goes way beyond it all. You can study biology and human genetics, and know everything there is to know about fertilization, reproduction, pregnancy, birth and childhood; but when you see your own new-born child, and two eyes meet yours with a look that seems to say, not 'Who are you?' but 'So – it's you!' you glimpse a mystery which no physical explanation can ever begin to explore.

It's the same with music. The physicist can in principle explain what happens when a particular instrument is played. But why Mozart makes us want to laugh and cry and dance, why some music is deeply consoling and some deeply disturbing, remains a mystery.

The deepest mysteries of human life – love, death, joy, beauty and the rest – have for millennia been believed to point to the deepest mystery of them all, the mystery of God. Sometimes in

1

the ancient world people developed whole systems for trying to penetrate this mystery, often in relation to a particular divinity such as Isis or Mithras. People believed that by going through particular initiation rites and disciplines they would get to the heart of the mystery, and would discover things that would change their lives completely.

Most Jews believed that the one true God had already invited them to share his own life and purpose, so they didn't go down this route. But they, too, knew a strong sense of mystery as they tried to understand the truth about how and why God had made the world, and in particular what his purpose was for them and for the future. Among the writings of ancient Israel, both in the Bible and in other books, there are many which try to penetrate to this truth, to discover what was going on in God's world, and where different people might fit into his purposes.

This is where Paul comes in. He picked up this Jewish tradition and declared that God's past, present and future had at last been unveiled in and through Jesus the Messiah. Jesus was the clue to all the secrets of God. Paul spells this out elsewhere, for instance in Colossians 1.26—2.3. And Paul wants the muddled Corinthian Christians to see that, though the message about the crucified Jesus is indeed a foolish, scandalous thing in the eyes of the rest of the world, at the heart of the Christian message there is the clue to the deepest mystery of life. In speaking like this, here in verse 7, and elsewhere, Paul may be teasing them a little about the way their culture and philosophy liked to probe into 'mysteries' of the pagan sort. He is pulling them over onto solidly Jewish ground.

One of the reasons, in fact, why the mystery of the gospel *is* a mystery is because nobody in Corinth or most other places would ever think of looking for the secret to life, the universe, God, beauty, love and death in a place of execution outside a rebellious city in the Middle East. Crucifixion was regarded in the ancient world as so horrible, so revolting, so degrading that you didn't mention it in polite society. Imagine somebody at a fashionable dinner-party going on in a loud voice about how he'd seen rats eating the body of a dead dog in the street; that's the kind of impression you'd make by standing up in public and talking about someone being crucified. No self-respecting sophist or rhetorician would dream of doing it. But Paul believed, and the new-found faith and life of the Corinthian Christians bore this out, that this was the clue to the mystery of life.

GOD'S STRANGE WISDOM

1 Corinthians 2.6–13

[6]We do, however, speak wisdom among the mature. But this isn't a wisdom of this present world, or of the rulers of this present world – those same rulers who are being done away with. [7]No: we speak God's hidden wisdom in a mystery. This is the wisdom God prepared ahead of time, before the world began, for our glory.

[8]None of the rulers of this present age knew about this wisdom. If they had, you see, they wouldn't have crucified the Lord of glory. [9]But, as the Bible says,

Human eyes have never seen,
human ears have never heard,
it's never entered human hearts:
all that God has now prepared
for those who truly love him –

[10]and that's what God has revealed to us through the spirit! The spirit, you see, searches everything, yes, even the depths of God. [11]Think of it this way: who knows what is really going on inside a person, except the spirit of the person which is inside them? Well, it's like that with God. Nobody knows what is going on inside God except God's spirit. [12]And we haven't received the spirit of the world, but the spirit that comes from

3

God, so that we can know the things that have been given to us by God.

[13]That, then, is what we speak. We don't use words we've been taught by human wisdom, but words we've been taught by the spirit, interpreting spiritual things to spiritual people.

When my sister celebrated her twenty-first birthday, she and I were at university, a long way from home. So a cousin of my father's, who lived nearby, invited the two of us to dinner to celebrate. He and his wife had no children of their own, and were eager to entertain us properly.

We had a wonderful meal and a delightful evening. As it drew towards a close, he produced the final touch. He had a bottle of brandy that was then 100 years old. He had been keeping it for a special occasion. He solemnly opened it, and poured everyone a glass. We sipped it equally solemnly, and told him how wonderful it was. We were truly grateful, but our praise meant nothing; we had neither of us ever tasted brandy before, and would not have been able to tell the difference between the contents of that bottle and a cheap one produced the previous week.

Paul speaks in this passage of a kind of teaching that is only for those who have grown up, who are mature, who have had their palates trained up from childish food and drink to appreciate and value the higher things. Having insisted that his gospel was, and needed to be, foolishness to Greeks and a scandal to Jews, he doesn't want them to think that this is all he has to offer. He really does have wisdom in store, deep and rich and many-sided; but it's only for those who can and will appreciate it, who are sufficiently grown-up in their spiritual discernment.

This is not to take back with the left hand what he's just given with the right. He doesn't mean that when converts get more mature he will then give them the same kind of 'wisdom' that you'd get from the sophists and philosophers in the wider world. Far from it. The wisdom he has in mind doesn't belong to 'this age' at all. It belongs to the 'age to come'; speaking of it to those who aren't already part of this 'age to come' is like speaking of a sunrise to blind people. Only those who have believed in the rising of the son of God can even begin to understand what this wisdom is. For the rest, it is as mad as the gospel itself.

Paul here draws on a crucial distinction. This, indeed, is one of the main things he wants the Corinthians to learn. World history divides into two 'ages' or epochs. There is the 'present age', the period of history characterized by human rebellion, sin, despair and death. Then there is 'the age to come', the time when the one true God will be king over all the world, bringing to an end the rule of all forces that oppose him. And the point is this: 'the age to come' has already broken in to the present age in Jesus the Messiah. His death and resurrection form the decisive break, the moment when the great melody of history has begun to be heard in a major key instead of a minor one.

That's why the present age, and its rulers, don't understand this wisdom. They are still playing the tune in the old key, and the notes of the gospel, and the new 'wisdom' that flows from it, simply won't fit. 'The rulers of this age' are clearly the actual governments of the world. They are the ones, Paul says, who 'crucified the Lord of glory' (verse 8): in other words, they are the political powers, and the actual rulers, who conspired to put Jesus on the cross. Rome, under the emperor Tiberius, was in charge, acting through the local governor, Pontius Pilate. Judaism, under the rule of the chief priests, in an uneasy relationship with Herod Antipas, 'the king of the Jews', played their part by keeping the local people on side with Rome's decision.

Thus, as my teacher, Professor George Caird, used to say, the highest religion and the best government that the world had ever seen got together to execute the Lord of glory – an irony that Paul, too, undoubtedly appreciated. The Bible is always clear that God intends human society to be ruled by appropriate wise and just government; but all government, precisely because it wields power, has the capacity to go bad, to become arrogant, to act in ways that promote its own self-interest instead of true justice, wisdom and truth. That, it appears, is what happened at Jesus' crucifixion. The ruling authorities had no thought that they were doing anything but getting rid of another trouble-maker, all in a day's work for ruthless empires from that day to this. But if they'd realized what was going on they would never have dreamed of doing such a thing. Why not? Not simply because they would have respected Jesus and refused to kill him. Rather, because they would have realized that in doing so they were signing their own death warrants.

In Colossians 2.15 Paul speaks, with heavy irony, of the cross of Jesus as the moment when the 'principalities and powers' were led along like a defeated rabble behind the chariot of a conquering general. Here in 1 Corinthians he speaks of Jesus winning the final victory over every rule and power and authority on the day when he finally appears as king (15.23–28). The two moments are closely joined together. What the cross achieves, the final 'appearing' of Jesus will implement fully. And if, as he says, the last enemy to be destroyed is death itself, the rulers of this world have nothing more to say. As every tyrant knows, death is the final threat by which power is exercised in this world.

Paul allows this statement about the ignorance of the present world rulers to hover in the air over what is to come. Their power is already doomed, and Christians are called to live as citizens of God's sovereign rule instead. For the moment, he develops the positive side: God has prepared for 'those who love him' (an Old Testament way of describing God's people) things which not only pass human wisdom and understanding but also imagination itself. (The quotation here is not from the Old Testament itself, but from another ancient Jewish book, known to some in the early church but now lost.) 'Wisdom', it turns out, is not just intellectual information, or even the elegance and beauty of abstract theories; it blossoms like a garden, flows like a mighty river, satisfies human beings at every level in ways we can't even guess at the moment. That is what God has in mind for those who love him.

How do we know? Because God has given us his spirit. Paul relishes the fact that the spirit who is poured out upon believers, bringing them to faith and opening their hearts and minds to the wisdom of the 'age to come', is God's own spirit, not some lesser being. The spirit within a person– the deep innermost life where thought, feeling, memory and imagination meet – knows best what the person is really all about. Even so, Paul declares, God's spirit is like that with God; and this spirit is given to all God's people in the Messiah.

This is an astonishing claim. It clearly doesn't mean that Christians automatically know everything about God, or why would Paul bother to write letters? It means that they have open access to God's mind – or, as he says in verse 16, to 'the mind of the Messiah'. But to explore this they must themselves be 'mature' (verse 6). They must themselves be, in some important sense which he will now go on to explain, 'spiritual'.

This tight-packed and challenging passage has many lessons for us, but perhaps the most important is for Christians who have forgotten, or perhaps never known, two truths.

The first is that there is a wealth of knowledge and life-enhancing understanding waiting for us to explore. Christianity is not simply a set of beliefs and a rule-book for life, such as anyone could master in a weekend. It is as many-sided as the world itself, full of beauty and mystery and power, and as terrifying and wonderful as God himself. There is always much, much more to learn, to relish, to delight in.

The second is that the Christian message from the very beginning challenged the world of power, including social and political power, with the message of God's superior kingdom unveiled in Jesus' death and resurrection. Paul doesn't want the Corinthians to imagine that he is talking simply about a religious experience that won't have anything to do with the real life of politics and government. He wouldn't want us to imagine that either. Let us not settle for a gospel which allows the world's power-games to proceed without challenge.

SPIRITUAL OR MERELY HUMAN?

1 Corinthians 2.14—3.4

[14]Someone living at the merely human level doesn't accept the things of God's spirit. They are foolishness to such people, you see, and they can't understand them because they need to be discerned spiritually. [15]But spiritual people discern everything, while nobody else can discern the truth about them! [16]For 'Who has known the mind of the Lord, so as to instruct him?' But we have the mind of the Messiah.

[3.1]In my own case, my dear family, I couldn't speak to you as spiritual people, but as people who were all too obviously merely human, little babies in the Messiah. [2]I fed you with milk, not solid food, because you weren't able to take it – and you still can't, even now! [3]You're still determined to live in the old way! Yes, wherever there is jealousy and quarrelling, doesn't that mean you're living in the old way, behaving as any merely human being might do? [4]When someone says 'I'm with Paul!', and someone else says 'I'm with Apollos!', are you not mere humans?

Once, during the 'hippy' era in the late 1960s, I sang and played my guitar in a folk club on the west side of Vancouver. I was there a week, and got to know some of the other regular performers quite well. One was a young man with the beginnings of a drug habit. He was quite a good guitarist, and a passable singer. But, some way into the evening, he would take a shot of whichever drug it was he was using at the time.

The effect was revealing. (I had never been remotely tempted to try drugs before, and I certainly didn't want to after watching him.) Once he was 'high', his playing and singing got worse and worse; but he came off stage convinced that he had been absolutely brilliant. Nothing could deter him from taking the drug to enhance his performance, as he thought, even though the rest of us tried to tell him it was doing the opposite.

Paul is now bringing his discussion of wisdom and folly, and spiritual maturity and immaturity, right down to where the Corinthians themselves are. They have been using the drug of sophistry, supposing it makes them more 'spiritual'; and Paul declares that it has made them all the more merely human.

They may by now have become fascinated by what he's been saying. Hearing the letter to this point, they will perhaps have been glad that he seems to have forgotten, or left behind, the issue he started with in Chapter 1 (the faction-fighting in support of different teachers). If they are thinking that, they are in for a shock; because the discussion about wisdom and maturity was all preparing the way to come back to the point. They have been imagining that they had a 'wisdom' which elevated them above the ordinary. They were eager for the kind of teaching the sophists were giving, imagining that by putting together a bit of Christian faith with a strong dose of sophistry they were becoming some kind of super-people. But they are deceived. The more they take the drug, the more immature they show themselves to be; and the proof of it all is – their in-fighting about different Christian teachers!

That is the main point Paul is making here, and it bears reflection in today's church as we so easily lapse from serious issues to personality-clashes, and from personalities to mere gossip, while all the time pretending we are still dealing with important matters. But we need to note as well the way in which Paul sets up the problem.

He begins by making the distinction between 'spiritual' people, the ones he's just mentioned in verse 13, the ones who can understand the deep and spiritual wisdom that as a teacher he longs to share with people, and 'merely human' people, people living on the ordinary level.

The word he uses which we translate 'merely human' is a tricky one. Other writers of the time use it in a variety of ways. Paul may himself be picking it up from things the Corinthians, or others, are saying, in order to turn it back and make it serve his purpose rather than theirs. But the basic difference he is describing is between people in whom God's spirit has come to dwell, opening them up to new depths and dimensions of truth and experience, and people who are living as though the world, and human life, was rumbling along in the same old way. They may think they're very sophisticated, but in reality they are 'merely human'.

The word he actually uses could be translated 'soul-ish' as opposed to 'spiritual' – meaning someone who is directed and led simply by the ordinary human interior life ('soul') rather than by the fresh, gospel-driven wisdom or energy given by God's spirit. Such a person (2.14) simply can't understand what's going on when the talk turns to the deeper things of the spirit. They become like a tone-deaf person at an opera: it's all nonsense to them. Take that picture one step further. Imagine being the only musical person listening to a wonderful string quartet in a large room full of tone-deaf people. That is rather like Paul's picture of being a 'spiritual' person in a world of 'merely human' people.

This could sound as though Paul is setting himself up as some kind of high and mighty spiritual leader, but that's not the point. He stresses first that the 'spiritual' person makes judgments on a different plane to the merely natural one (verse 15), while the judgments that such people make will pass him or her by without effect. The evidence he offers is a quotation from Isaiah 40.13, where the prophet looks at the wider world and asks, 'Who has known YHWH's mind?', expecting the answer, 'No one'. But if the Messiah has already become for us 'wisdom, righteousness, sanctification and redemption' (1.30), then it is not a long step to say that we – that is, those who have the spirit – possess the Messiah's *mind*. If that is true, there is no depth of wisdom too deep, no height too high, for us to explore.

But the Corinthians themselves aren't ready for it! Paul shakes his head over them. They may have supposed, listening to the letter as it is read out in their assembly, that he is talking about them as the 'spiritual' ones, but he isn't. He uses the language many teachers of his day employed to explain the difference between those who were ready for serious teaching and those who were still at the infancy stage. When he had been with them before, he explains, he only taught them the basics: milk, not meat. He may be answering the charge that his teaching had been very basic; the other teachers who'd come in after him had been much more exciting, much deeper, much more gratifying to the Corinthian eagerness for social and spiritual status and pride . . .

. . . which only goes to show, Paul concludes, that you are still babies, even now (3.1–2)! You are driven by all-too-human impulses. Here again Paul uses words which are difficult to translate, but which mean, more or less, 'living on the basis of your created and corruptible nature alone' (verse 1), and 'living as people determined to make that created and corruptible nature alone your guide and rule' (verse 3). There is, in fact, a very subtle shift from 'merely human' (2.14) to 'all too obviously human' (3.1), to 'very determinedly only-human' (i.e. actually resisting the spirit, not merely showing no evidence of it) (3.3). Paul is not suggesting that each of these words refers to a different level of Christian (or sub-Christian) experience, or to a different type of person. He is insisting that all of them alike are 'unspiritual' – and that the Corinthian church, insofar as it is indulging in personality cults, is showing strong evidence of exactly that.

EVERYTHING BELONGS TO YOU

1 Corinthians 3.18–23

[18]Don't let anyone deceive themselves. If anyone among you supposes they are wise in the present age, let them become foolish, so that they can become wise. [19]The wisdom of this world, you see, is folly with God. This is what the Bible says: 'He catches the wise in their trickery.' [20]And again, 'The Lord knows the thinking of the wise – and he knows that it's all a sham!'

[21]So don't let anyone boast about mere human beings. For everything belongs to you, [22]whether it's Paul or Apollos or Cephas, whether it's the world or life or death, whether it's the present or the future – everything belongs to you! [23]And you belong to the Messiah; and the Messiah belongs to God.

I remember a wise address given at a graduation ceremony by a respected senior professor. (I was present in order to say the opening prayer.) In his address, the great man said many things, and gave a lot of good advice, but the one thing that stands out in my memory is his description of a humble faith. 'It isn't', he said, 'a matter of knowing that you've got it all together; you haven't. It's a matter of knowing that somewhere it *is* all together – and that you're part of it.'

That combination of humility and confidence is hard to keep in balance. The pressure from the world around us is always trying to make us either deny that we know anything or adopt one of those brittle, high-risk, know-it-all positions. Genuine Christian faith isn't like that. It involves learning to be foolish, as Paul says here, in order to become wise; and it involves celebrating that fact that 'all things are yours' while recognizing that 'you belong to the Messiah; and the Messiah belongs to God'. What does Paul mean by these astonishing statements?

He is rounding off the central part of his argument about the danger of 'boasting' about human beings – the danger into which the Corinthian church has fallen with a splash. They had been saying 'I belong to Paul', 'I belong to Apollos', and so on, setting up Paul and the other Christian teachers as 'owners' of groups of disciples, after the manner of the sophists and 'wisdom' teachers of the day. But, in addition to all the other things that were wrong with their attitude, Paul's word here is that such a position is actually selling themselves short. It isn't that they belong to these teachers; rather, all these teachers belong to *them*! In fact, not only the teachers belong to them, but everything else does as well – excepting only the Messiah, and of course God himself! What can he be thinking of?

It makes sense only within the world of Jewish thought, according to which those who belong to God's true people are destined, when the 'age to come' is fully here, to rule the world in obedience to God. As the book of Revelation puts it, adapting an ancient promise to Israel, God's people are to be 'kings and priests' in the new world (Revelation 1.6; see Exodus 19.6).

There were, of course, pagan philosophies which taught people that they were in some sense 'kings' already, if only they could learn to master themselves and discover their true place in the world. But Paul's promise, building on the Jewish tradition, goes way beyond what was on offer in the world at large. The apostles belong to you! The apostles don't own the church; instead, as Paul has said a few verses ago, they are the property of the church, 'servants through whom you believed' (verse 5). But it isn't just the apostles; it's the world itself. Paul is no dualist, rejecting the created world as evil; the God who revealed himself in and as Jesus of Nazareth is the same God who made the world, and by belonging to him Christians inherit the world, as Jesus himself declared (Matthew 5.5; Paul says in 1 Corinthians 6.2 that God's people will *judge* the world).

And, if the world, then life and death themselves. Christians are, in other words, already resurrection people, because of the sure hope that is theirs through the gospel message of Jesus' own resurrection (chapter 15). The present and the future belong to them; that's how important they already are. They are assured, even while the 'present evil age' is continuing, that they belong in 'the age to come'. Nor do they belong in it as 'extras', coming in alongside in a script that is basically about someone or something else. They are the stars of the show.

In short, the Corinthians were like people splashing about in a muddy pool when the ocean itself was right beside them; like people drinking dirty water from a polluted tap when the finest wine, and sparkling mountain water, were theirs to command. Fancy indulging in personality cults, as though you were merely another bunch of squabbling sophists, when the entire cosmos and all its truth, mystery and wisdom were yours for the exploring! Temptations often promise more and give less – sometimes, in fact, nothing at all. Satan offers the moon, and then laughs at you when you don't get it, while God promises you the sun itself.

It is vital to get everything in the right order. Paul develops in several passages a way of talking about the Messiah and God in the same breath. This enables him to declare at the same time, first, that Jesus, the Messiah, is on God's side of the picture over against the whole world and the rest of the human race, and, second, that Jesus remains distinct from the God whom elsewhere he calls 'the father' or 'the creator'. Paul didn't take the time to write a long treatise about how this might all work out philosophically. He didn't need to. Enough to state, again and again as he does, that when Christians look up from the world, and from their own lives, they see, not a distant or unapproachable deity, not a vague divine force that they couldn't know much about, but the God of Israel, the creator God, who has made himself known in Jesus.

The point is that you don't have to understand how it all works. You have to believe – on the evidence of Jesus' resurrection in particular – *that* it works, and that you are called to be part of it. And believing that is itself, Paul would say, the sign that God's spirit, the spirit of God's son Jesus, is living within you, making you part of his Temple, the people whose primary task it is to worship and praise him.

That's why all human wisdom is overturned by the divine folly of the gospel. Verses 18–20 sum up, and buttress with further biblical quotations, the point Paul has been making from various angles ever since 1.18. And the sharp command which goes with this summing-up, which we need today as much as ever, is this: don't deceive yourself (verse 18). It is easy to do, and the results are sad. And those who think they're not likely to deceive themselves are the very ones who are about to do so.

THE CHALLENGE OF FAITH

James 1.2–8

²My dear family, when you find yourselves tumbling into various trials and tribulations, learn to look at it with complete joy, ³because you know that, when your faith is put to the test, what comes out is patience. ⁴What's more, you must let patience have its complete effect, so that you may be complete and whole, not falling short in anything.

⁵If any one of you falls short in wisdom, they should ask God for it, and it will be given them. God, after all, gives generously and ungrudgingly to all people. ⁶But they should ask in faith, with no doubts. A person who doubts is like a wave of the sea which the wind blows and tosses about. ⁷Someone like that should not suppose they will receive anything from the Lord, ⁸since they are double-minded and unstable in everything they do.

I used to think the waves had come from far away. Standing by the sea and watching the grey-green monsters roll in, it was easy to imagine that this wave, and then this one, and then the one after that, had made the journey from a distant land. Here they were, like the Magi, arriving at last to deposit their gifts.

But of course it isn't like that. Waves are what happens when wind and tide take hold of the waters that are there all the time and make them dance to their tune. Just yesterday I stood in the bright sunshine and watched them sparkling and splashing around a little harbour, making the boats dip and bob. A fine sight; the waves seem to have character and energy of their own. But they don't. They are the random products of other forces.

The challenge of faith is the challenge not to be a wave. There are many winds and tides in human life, and it's easy to imagine ourselves important because we seem, from time to time at least, to dance and sparkle this way and that. The question is whether the character that develops within us is the real thing, or whether, as James says in verse 6, we are simply double-minded and unstable, blown and tossed about by this wind or that.

When a Christian is tested it shows something real is happening. There are many kinds of test: actual persecution, which many face today; fierce and nasty temptations, which can strike suddenly when we're not expecting them; physical sickness or bereavement; family or financial troubles; and so on. But you wouldn't be tested unless you were doing something serious. Mechanics don't test scrap metal; they test cars that are going to face tough conditions. Those who follow Jesus the Messiah are not simply supposed to survive. They are supposed to count, to make a difference in the world, whether through the quiet daily witness of a faithful and gentle life or the chance, given to some, to speak and act in a way which reveals the gospel to many others. For all of that we need to become strong, to face up to the challenge.

So James draws attention to the result of the test: patience. Don't panic. Don't over-react. Don't turn a problem into a crisis. Be patient. And, says James, you should let patience have its complete effect. Let it work right through your system (verse 4). Imagine your life like a house. Faith is what happens when you look out of the window, away from yourself, to the God who is so much greater than you. Patience is what happens inside the house when you do that.

One of the other great themes of James comes here at the beginning, in parallel with patience. Wisdom! James is the most obvious representative in the New Testament of what in the ancient Israelite scriptures (the Old Testament) we think of as 'wisdom literature': the sifted, tested and collected wisdom of those who learned to trust God for everything and to discover how that trust would work out in every aspect of daily life. How should I cope with this situation, with that tricky moment? You need wisdom – and you should ask for it.

But how do I know that God will give it to me? Here, as the secret of faith, patience and wisdom combined, we have the heart of what James wants to say. God gives generously and ungrudgingly to all people (verse 5). How easy it is for us to imagine that God is stingy and mean. We project on to the maker of all things the fearful, petty or even spiteful character we meet so often in real life, sometimes even when we look in the mirror. Learning who God really is and what he's truly like – and reminding ourselves of it regularly – is the key to it all. Without that, you'll be double-minded, swept this way one minute and that way the next. You'll just be another wave. With it, you will have a settled character. Wisdom. Patience. Faith.

TRUE AND FALSE WISDOM

James 3.13–18

[13]Who is wise and discerning among you? Such a person should, by their upright behaviour, display their works in the humility of wisdom. [14]But if you have bitter jealousy and contention in your hearts, don't boast, and tell lies against the truth. [15]This isn't the wisdom that comes from above. It is earthly, merely human, coming from the world of demons. [16]For where

17

there is jealousy and contention, there you will get unruly behaviour and every kind of evil practice. [17]But the wisdom that comes from above is first holy, then peaceful, gentle, compliant, filled with mercy and good fruits, unbiased, sincere. [18]And the fruit of righteousness is sown in peace by those who make peace.

It all began with a wrong diagnosis. I came upon the obituary of a famous actress in the newspaper just the other day. She wasn't particularly old – in her early 70s, quite young these days. Her doctor hadn't seen the early warning signs. By the time she complained of a pain it was too late. The disease had spread, and she had only months to live.

It's a sad story, repeated of course countless times, even with all the medical advances we now have. It is possible for someone to imagine they are perfectly healthy when they are walking around with something unpleasant eating away at them inside.

That is what James is talking about here. He isn't, of course, referring here to physical illness – though the sickness in question can sometimes go with actual physical ill-health. It may sometimes be difficult to say which causes which. What he is talking about is 'bitter jealousy and contention', a spirit which is always carping and criticizing, which cannot let a nice word go by without adding a nasty one, to take the taste away (as it were). And when someone with that kind of spirit claims to be healthy – claims, for instance, to be a practising Christian – James has a sharp response. Such a person, he says, is boasting. They are telling lies against the truth (verse 14).

The diagnosis goes deeper still. He has already said that the tongue is a fire set aflame by hell; now (verse 15) he says that a mindset like that comes from the world of demons. It may give some appearance of wisdom. Cynicism often does. Well, you wouldn't expect a demonic mindset to identify itself too obviously, would you?

We are faced, then, with two kinds of wisdom. This may well be a word for our day, when so many people across the world are fed up with the way their country is run, with the way their police force behaves, with the way the global economy functions, and so on. Often these criticisms are fully justified, as they certainly would have been in James's own day. But the challenge then for God's people is to be able to tell the truth about the way the world is, and about the way wicked people are behaving, without turning into a perpetual grumble, and in particular without becoming someone whose appearance of 'wisdom' consists in being able to find a cutting word to say about everyone and everything. There is still, after all, a vast amount of beauty, love, generosity and sheer goodness in the world. Those who follow Jesus ought not only to be celebrating it but contributing to it. It's better, as the saying goes, to light a candle than to curse the darkness.

Jesus himself had declared a special blessing on 'peacemakers', and James picks that up here (verse 18). Allowing a jealous spirit to spill out into fault-finding and backbiting is not only not making peace. It is allowing the build-up of a climate of fear, anger and suspicion in which wars and fightings can all too easily occur.

So what's the answer? In the middle of these warnings, James offers in verse 17 a lovely, though compact, description of 'the wisdom that comes from above'. It's clear that this 'wisdom' isn't a matter of knowing a large number of facts. Nor is it a particular skill in negotiating, or managing, or leadership, or academic scholarship. It is much deeper than any of these. It is 'holy, peaceful, gentle, compliant, filled with mercy and good fruits, unbiased, sincere'. It might be easy for those James has described already, those filled with jealousy and contention, to pour scorn on these characteristics. In our cynical age people might look on someone who is gentle and compliant as a wimp, perhaps a bit naive, not really aware of how nasty the world is.

But these characteristics have nothing to do with naivety. They are hard to acquire and hard to maintain. They can only be sustained at great personal cost. They only appear where there has been a steady habit of prayer and self-discipline; even then they may take a while to show themselves. It would be worth spending the time to work through the words in this list one by one. Do it slowly. Review your life in the light of them. You might want to make a note of the times, the places, and particularly the people, that make it hard for you to live in this way – and then to pray for strength, and for this wisdom from above, to hold firm when the challenge comes round once more.

Think of it like this. Suppose you lived in a village, or worked in a college, or a factory, or a farm. Suppose some of the people you met every day were like the people in verse 16, and others like the people in verse 17. Which one would you rather see coming towards you down the street? Which one would you rather have as a neighbour? The question answers itself. The challenge is how to become that neighbour yourself. And once more the answer is this. Wisdom comes 'from above'. Pray for it. Persevere.

2

THE TRANSFORMATION OF THE SELF

THE LIVING SACRIFICE
Romans 12.1–2

> [1]So, my dear family, this is my appeal to you by the mercies of God: offer your bodies as a living sacrifice, holy and pleasing to God. Worship like this brings your mind into line with God's. [2]What's more, don't let yourselves be squeezed into the shape dictated by the present age. Instead, be transformed by the renewing of your minds, so that you can work out what God's will is, what is good, acceptable and complete.

William was coming to the end of his first year as chairman of the company when I met him at a lunch.

'How's it been going?' I asked.

'Oh,' he said, 'it's been wonderful in several ways. The company is doing well and I'm proud to be part of it.'

'Why only several ways?' I asked, picking up the implied hesitation in the way he had answered.

'Well,' he said, 'I've only just realized what my problem has been. Everybody in the company has a clear idea of how they want the chairman to act, what sort of meetings they think they need, and so on. I've done my best to make my number with everyone. I've gone out of my way to learn the procedures they have in place. But I've figured out now that I've gone too far. I've let their expectations dictate the shape of my work, of how I spend my time. I now need to turn that inside out. I have my own ideas of what we should be doing, and from now on I'm going to set the pace.'

Now, of course, a wise executive will want to listen carefully to those who know more about the company than he or she does. To this extent the picture doesn't quite fit what Paul is saying. But it does in the all-important point: his appeal now is that we should refuse to let 'the present age' squeeze us into its mould, dictate to us how we should think and indeed *what* we should think, and tell us how we can and can't behave. Instead, we are to be transformed; our minds need to be renewed. We have to set the pace ourselves, and work out what sort of people we should be. The basis for this is not what the surrounding culture expects of us, but what God in his mercy has done for us.

One of the key phrases here is 'the present age' (verse 2). In Galatians 1.4 Paul calls this 'the present *evil* age'. Like many first-century Jews, he believed that world history was divided into 'the present age', characterized by rebellion against God and the corruption and death which result, and 'the age to come', in which God would give new life to the world and humankind, bringing justice, joy and peace once and for all. Part of the point of Paul's gospel is his belief that this 'age to come' had already begun in Jesus, and supremely in his death and resurrection.

Christians are therefore in the position, not (to be sure) of a new executive learning the job, but of someone who needs to stop letting the world around dictate its own terms and conditions, and who instead must figure out how to think, speak and act as is appropriate not for the present age but for the new age which is already breaking in. Christians are called to be counter-cultural – not in all respects, as though every single aspect of human society and culture were automatically and completely bad, but at least in being prepared to think through each aspect of life. We must be ready to challenge those parts where the present age shouts, or perhaps whispers seductively, that it would be easier and better to do things *that* way, while the age to come, already begun in Jesus, insists that belonging to the new creation means that we must live *this* way instead.

The key to it all is the transforming of the *mind*. Many Christians in today's world never come to terms with this. They hope they will be able to live up to something like Christian standards while still thinking the way the rest of the world thinks. It can't be done. Paul's analysis of human rebellion against God in Romans 1.18–32 includes a fair amount of wrong *thinking*. Having the mind renewed by the persuasion of the spirit is the vital start of that true human living which is God's loving will for all his children.

This, after all, is a way of growing up to maturity. People sometimes suggest that living a Christian life means a kind of immaturity, since you are guided not by thinking things through for yourself but by rules and regulations derived from elsewhere. That isn't Paul's vision of Christian living. Of course there are plenty of firm boundaries. But at the centre of genuine Christianity is a mind awake, alert, not content to take a few guidelines off the peg but determined to understand *why* human life is meant to be lived in one way rather than another. In fact, it is the way of life of 'the present age' which often involves the real human immaturity, as people simply look at the surrounding culture, with all its shallow and silly patterns of behaviour, and copy it unthinkingly.

For Paul, the mind and the body are closely interconnected, and must work as a coherent team. Having one's mind renewed and offering God one's body (verse 1) are all part of the same complete event. Here Paul uses a vivid, indeed shocking, idea: one's whole self (that's what Paul means by 'body') must be laid on the altar like a sacrifice in the Temple. The big difference is that, whereas the sacrifice is there to be killed, the Christian's self-offering is actually all about coming alive with the new life that bursts out in unexpected ways once the evil deeds of the self are put to death. Christian living never begins with a set of rules, though it contains them as it goes forwards. It begins in the glad self-offering of one's whole self to the God whose mercy has come all the way to meet us in our rebellion, sin and death. Within that, it involves the renewal of the mind so that we are enabled both to think straight, instead of the twisted thinking that the world would force upon us, and to act accordingly.

FRUIT OF THE SPIRIT
Galatians 5.22–26

[22]The fruit of the spirit is love, joy, peace, great-heartedness, kindness, generosity, faithfulness, [23]gentleness, self-control. There is no law that opposes things like that! [24]And those who belong to the Messiah, Jesus, crucified the flesh with its passions and desires. [25]If we live by the spirit, let's line up with the spirit. [26]We shouldn't be conceited, vying with one another and jealous of each other.

The Christmas decorations were spectacular. I went down the street from store to store, and in each window – and indeed in the street itself – there were pretty lights and multicoloured decorations. Every shop seemed to have sparkling trees, alive with parcels, bells, fairies, glass balls, and all kinds of trinkets and decorations.

Or at least, they looked alive. In reality, of course, they weren't. It was all a show. I went down the same street a month later, as the decorations were being taken down. It was very bleak. The tinsel and coloured balls went back into boxes. The trees were either folded up (they weren't real, after all) or thrown out. Nothing had actually been growing on them. It looked magnificent, but it was all artificial.

If Paul is famous for his contrast of 'flesh' and 'spirit', he is also famous for the key words he uses that go with them both. He speaks of the *works* of the 'flesh', but the *fruit* of the 'spirit'. Compare those Christmas trees for a minute with ordinary, humdrum but real fruit trees in an orchard. The Christmas trees look wonderful for a short while, but then they get packed away or thrown out. The fruit trees may not look so spectacular, but if they're properly cared for they will go on bearing fruit year after year. Which is more important? You hardly have to ask.

Underneath the two lists – the works of the flesh and the fruit of the spirit – there lies Paul's whole vision of what happens to someone when they come, through faith and baptism, into the community of the Messiah's people. (Notice how, in verse 24, he speaks of Christians as 'those who belong to the Messiah'; and how he assumes, as he does in 4.4–7, that all such people are indwelt by the spirit.) There are various stages to be observed, which he condenses here.

People start off in the condition he calls 'flesh'. They are born into human families, with ethnic and territorial identities. They discover within themselves all kinds of desires, which, if allowed full rein, will produce the 'works' listed in 5.19–21. A glance back at this list will reveal that a society in which most people behaved in such a way is unlikely to be a happy or thriving place. What is more, when God finally establishes his kingdom, people like that will have no place in it; it would be very surprising if they did. That's not the sort of place, and state of affairs, that God wishes ultimately to create.

But then, through the announcement of the gospel of Jesus, God's spirit goes to work and people are renewed. The first sign of that renewal, and hence the true badge of their belonging, is their faith in Jesus as the risen Lord. But their membership in the Messiah's people involves them in a movement through death to new life. What is left behind in this death, this co-crucifixion with the Messiah, is precisely the life in which 'the flesh' determines who one is and how one behaves.

Instead, they begin to 'bear fruit'. The nine qualities Paul lists in verses 22–23 are not things which, if we try hard enough, we could simply do without help, without the spirit. If you suspect that someone who is being kind to you is having to try very hard to do it, the kindness itself loses its flavour. The point of all of them is that when the spirit is at work they will begin to happen; new motivations will appear.

Not, of course, that this process bypasses our thinking and willing. We have to set our minds and intentions to do them; it isn't a matter of just relaxing and doing what comes naturally. Otherwise Paul wouldn't need to urge the Galatians to 'line up with the spirit' (verse 25), that is, to see the effect the spirit wants to produce, to reflect on how it will come about, and through our own moral effort to let the life of the spirit have its complete way. But the point is that when these qualities appear, with all their quiet joy, all their rich contribution to the sort of community God intends and will eventually produce, they come like the fruit in an orchard, not like the baubles on a Christmas tree. They will truly be part of who we will have become.

OFF WITH THE OLD, ON WITH THE NEW
Ephesians 4.17–24

[17]So this is what I want to say; I am bearing witness to it in the Lord. You must no longer behave like the Gentiles, foolish-minded as they are. [18]Their understanding is darkened; they are cut off from God's life because of their deep-seated ignorance, which springs from the fact that their hearts are hard. [19]They have lost all moral sensitivity, and have given themselves over to whatever takes their fancy. They go off greedily after every kind of uncleanness.

[20]But that's not how you learned the king! – [21]if indeed you did hear about him, and were taught in him, in accordance with the truth about Jesus himself. [22]That teaching stressed that you should take off your former lifestyle, the old humanity. That way of life is decaying, as a result of deceitful lusts.

[23]Instead, you must be renewed in the spirit of your mind, [24]and you must put on the new humanity, which is being created the way God intended it, displaying justice and genuine holiness.

We couldn't understand why the agency was being so unhelpful.

We had answered the advertisement and were eager to rent the apartment that we had been offered. There were some minor problems, but nothing too difficult to sort out. But every time we telephoned we spoke to a different person, and they never seemed to understand what was happening. They gave different answers each time we asked the questions. They quoted us different rates. The worst thing was that they didn't really seem to care whether we rented the place or not.

When we finally visited the office it became clear. The secretaries and assistants we had been speaking to on the telephone were bright enough. They obviously would have liked to be helpful. But the manager – who had never talked to us himself – was impossible. He was inefficient, haphazard, and we suspected he had a drink problem. But he covered it all up by being a bully. He shouted at his employees and gave them different instructions every day. No wonder they hadn't been able to help us very much. Only by confronting him directly and making him face the issues could we begin to sort everything out.

When we begin to get to grips with the wrong way and the right way to live a truly human life, it's no good starting with the junior members of the establishment. People often suppose that Christian behaviour is simply a matter of getting your body to do certain things and not to do certain other things. That's like trying to do business with the assistants rather than with the incompetent manager. Paul makes it clear in this passage that you've got to go about it the other way round. And the incompetent manager isn't the human body. It's the human mind.

To be sure, Paul longs to see the young churches changing their behaviour. The pagan way of life all around them is deadly. But you can't alter behaviour without changing the mind; and the pagan, Gentile mind, he says, is foolish (verse 17), with darkened understanding and deep-seated ignorance (verse 18). This in turn springs from sheer hard-heartedness. A heart and mind like this produce moral insensitivity, the inability even to notice that some things are right and others are wrong. Once that's in place, anything goes (verse 19). You won't understand where the behaviour comes from unless you understand the state of heart and mind. And you won't *change* the behaviour unless you change the heart and mind.

This isn't what many people today expect to hear. There is a persistent untruth which has made its way into the popular imagination in our day: that Christianity means closing off your mind, ceasing all serious thought, and living in a shallow fantasy world divorced from the solid truths of 'real life'. Of course there are some Christians who try to live like that; and of course there are many non-Christians who use their minds in rich and varied ways. We mustn't simply reverse the popular stereotype.

But the truth is that genuine Christianity opens the mind so that it can grasp truth at deeper and deeper levels. This isn't a matter of university degrees and paper qualifications, helpful though they may be. It's a matter of the heart and mind being open to the ever wider range of insight and imagination that comes with 'learning the king' (verse 20).

This is one of the few places where Paul refers to the basic Christian teaching which he assumes new converts receive. His letters don't usually repeat this teaching, except on very rare occasions when a point needs rubbing in (e.g. 1 Corinthians 11.23–26). As a result, we are in the position of someone watching the sequel to a movie without seeing the original one. We have to work out from the letters, which are all written to people who have already become Christians and received basic teaching, what the original preaching and teaching consisted of. And here we have a clear indication: it has to do with Jesus himself.

Well, of course, you may think. What else would it be about? But many people have questioned whether Paul and his churches really knew much about Jesus himself, other than the fact that he was crucified, then raised to life, and now exalted as Lord of the world. But here Paul seems to envisage that part of the basic Christian teaching which converts in Asia Minor had received would include teaching on behaviour which came from Jesus himself. And since we have in the gospels teaching of just this sort – teaching which stresses that the human heart and mind are the source of evil behaviour, so that the heart itself needs to be changed (e.g. Mark 7.14–23) – we would be right to assume that this is what he has in mind.

So what Paul is urging the young Christians is that they allow this teaching of Jesus to have its full effect in their lives. Now that they are 'in Christ', they have the responsibility, in the power of the spirit, to take off the old lifestyle, the old way of being human, like someone stripping off a shabby and worn suit of clothing. It may have become comfortable. You may be used to it, and even quite like it. Familiar old clothes are often like that, and brand new ones often feel a bit strange. But if you want to live as a new person in and for the king, the old suit of clothes has to come off, and the new one has to go on.

The point, then, is not to be deceived by what lust and greed whisper in your ear. It's the mind and heart that matter. If they learn to recognize the deceitful whisperings, to name them and reject them, the first vital step to the new way of life has been taken. 'Be renewed in the spirit of your mind' (verse 23): that's the secret. If the heart is right, it's time to get the mind right. Then you'll have the energy of will-power to bring the behaviour into line. Off with the old, on with the new!

JOY AND PEACE IN GOD

Philippians 4.2–9

[2]I have a special appeal which goes jointly to Euodia and Syntyche: please, please, come to a common mind in the Lord. [3](And here's a request for you too, my loyal comrade: please help these women. They have struggled hard in the gospel alongside me, as have Clement and my other fellow-workers, whose names are in the book of life.)

[4]Celebrate joyfully in the Lord, all the time. I'll say it again: celebrate! [5]Let everybody know how gentle and gracious you are. The Lord is near.

[6]Don't worry about anything. Rather, in every area of life let God know what you want, as you pray and make requests, and give thanks as well. [7]And God's peace, which is greater than we can ever understand, will keep guard over your hearts and minds in King Jesus.

[8]For the rest, my dear family, these are the things you should think through: whatever is true, whatever is holy, whatever is upright, whatever is pure, whatever is attractive, whatever has a good reputation; anything virtuous, anything praiseworthy. [9]And these are the things you should do: what you learned, received, heard and saw in and through me. And the God of peace will be with you.

You never know when it's going to happen. Two people who one day are good friends, working alongside each other in the church or community, can suddenly get across each other. A sharp word from one, half-heard by the other; a bitter response, said hastily and without quite meaning it; then the slamming of doors, the face turned away in the street, the sense (on both sides) of hurt so great, and offence so deep, that nothing can mend it. I remember my grandfather, a pastor himself, telling me of such things. I in my turn have had to deal with a few such incidents, and I guess most pastors have done the same.

It is particularly sad and tragic when it occurs within a Christian community where the whole ethos ought to be one of mutual love, forgiveness and support; but the chances are that since each one will accuse the other of being the first to break this code, neither is prepared to back down. It then calls for a certain amount of what in international relations is called 'shuttle diplomacy' on the part of a pastor or wise friend before any progress is made.

But a word addressed in public to both parties might just break the deadlock (though you'd have to know what you were doing; it might make it worse). We assume from verse 2 that Paul knew what he was doing. Two women in Philippi, Euodia and Syntyche, have fallen out, and he's appealing publicly for them to come to agreement.

These things are better dealt with sooner rather than later. I was talking yesterday to a sensible lady, a mother and grand-mother, who told me that her golden rule was never to let more than two days' ironing pile up. After that it would be too daunting to contemplate. In the same way, something that needs to be ironed out within the Christian community should be tackled as quickly as possible, before resentment solidifies and cannot be softened and melted.

After this brief aside for a particular problem, Paul turns to his real final command. Everything comes under the great heading in verse 4: Celebrate in the Lord!

Often the word here is translated 'rejoice'. We normally under-stand that word today, I think, as meaning something that happens inside people, a sense of joy welling up and making them happy from within. All that is important, and is contained within Paul's command; but in his world and culture this rejoicing would have meant (what we would call) public celebration. The world all around, in Ephesus, Philippi, Corinth and elsewhere used to organize great festivals, games and shows to celebrate their gods and their cities, not least the new 'god', Caesar himself. Why shouldn't the followers of King Jesus celebrate exuberantly? It's only right; and celebrating Jesus as Lord encourages and strengthens loyalty and obedience to him.

At the same time, it's interesting that he at once says that the public image of the Christian church should be of a gentle, gracious community (verse 5). Exuberance must not turn into mere extrovert enthusiasm which squashes sensitive souls and offends those who are by nature quiet and reserved.

The three main things that will come into line if the celebration is both joyful and gentle are the prayer which overcomes anxiety (verses 6–7); the patterns of thought which celebrate God's goodness throughout creation (verse 8); and the style of life which embodies the gospel (verse 9).

Anxiety was a way of life for many in the ancient pagan world. With so many gods and goddesses, all of them potentially out to get you for some offence you mightn't even know about, you never knew whether something bad was waiting for you just round the corner. With the God who had now revealed himself in Jesus, there was no guarantee against suffering, but there was the certainty that this God was ultimately in control and that he would always hear and answer prayers on any topic whatsoever. People sometimes say today that one shouldn't bother God about trivial requests (fine weather for the church picnic; a parking space in a busy street); but, though of course our intercessions should normally focus on serious and major matters, we note that Paul says we should ask God about *every* area of life. If it matters to you, it matters to God. Prayer like that will mean that God's peace – not a Stoic lack of concern, but a deep peace in the middle of life's problems and storms – will keep guard around your heart and mind, like a squadron of soldiers looking after a treasure chest.

The command in verse 8, to think about all the wonderful and lovely things listed here, runs directly opposite to the habits of mind instilled by the modern media. Read the newspapers: their stock-in-trade is anything that is untrue, unholy, unjust, impure, ugly, of ill repute, vicious and blameworthy. Is that a true representation of God's good and beautiful world? How are you going to celebrate the goodness of the creator if you feed your mind only on the places in the world which humans have made ugly? How are you going to take steps to fill your mind instead with all the things that God has given us to be legitimately pleased with, and to enjoy and celebrate?

Finally, reflect for a moment on Paul's command in verse 9. It is one of the most demanding ethical commands anywhere in the Bible – not so much for those who receive it, though no doubt it's that as well, but for the person who gives it. Which of us could say, after staying in a town for a few weeks, that the way to be a good Christian was to do exactly what we ourselves had done?

As so often, Paul weaves into apparently brief and unconnected strands of thought a theme which turns, teasingly, this way and that. Where does 'the peace of God' come from (verse 7)? Why, from 'the God of peace', of course (verse 9). Get to know the one and you'll have the other.

DYING AND RISING WITH CHRIST
Colossians 2.20—3.4

[20]If you died with the king, coming out from the rule of the 'worldly elements', what's the point of laying down laws as though your life was still merely worldly? [21]'Don't handle! Don't taste! Don't touch!' [22]Rules like that all have to do with things

that disappear as you use them. They are the sort of regulations and teachings that mere humans invent. [23]They may give an appearance of wisdom, since they promote a do-it-yourself religion, a kind of humility, and severe treatment of the body. But they are of no use when it comes to dealing with physical self-indulgence.

[3.1]So if you were raised to life with the king, search for the things that are above, where the king is seated at God's right hand! [2]Think about the things that are above, not the things that belong on the earth. [3]Don't you see: you died, and your life has been hidden with the king, in God! [4]When the king is revealed (and he is your life, remember), then you too will be revealed with him in glory.

'I'll just be two minutes,' I said, leaving my friends on the street corner while I went to fetch the car. It was raining, and we'd just come out of the theatre.

But I wasn't two minutes. I took more like ten. They were starting to worry that I'd had an accident. I hadn't. I had driven out of the car park and tried to turn into the street where they were waiting for me. But I wasn't allowed to turn that way. There was a one-way system. I was forced to set off in exactly the opposite direction and to go a long, long way round through narrow, twisting and winding streets before I could find my way back. What looks like the shortest way is often impossible. Sometimes the correct way is what seems the hardest.

Paul is warning the Colossians about the dangers of being drawn into Judaism. But in this passage he's doing something else as well: he is showing them the way to a genuine, full-blooded holiness. It isn't what might seem the shortest, most obvious way; but it's the way that will bring them where they need to be.

One of the principal appeals of Judaism in the pagan world of the first century was its high moral code. It made heavy demands, and often when people are sick and tired of the murky and immoral world of paganism they are glad to embrace a way of life which offers clear, bright, clean lines. Serious-minded people in a place like Colossae, people who had begun to realize that their pagan gods weren't doing them any good, might well feel that the regulations of the Torah itself, and of the numerous explanatory additions that first-century teachers expounded, were going to be a great help to them in finding a new way of life that would leave the messy world of paganism behind once and for all. 'Don't handle this, don't taste that, don't touch this'; the very detail of the regulations, and the severe self-discipline needed to keep them, would make them feel they really must be making advances in their moral and spiritual lives.

Well, says Paul, it may feel like that, but it's an illusion. Go that way, and the street will soon come to a dead end. These are simply regulations that function at a worldly level. You will merely be giving up a worldly self-indulgence of a sensual kind for a worldly self-indulgence of a spiritual kind. A religion that focuses purely on the details of things you're allowed, or not allowed, to touch or eat – he obviously has the Jewish food regulations in mind – is dealing with perishables; and if you want to do business with God you have to get beyond that. In short, when Judaism sets itself against its own Messiah, it may well have the appearance of wisdom in the kind of religion it comes up with, but it won't actually attain the goal. It won't succeed in making you genuinely holy, through and through.

For that, you need to go what seems like a much harder and longer route, but it's the one that will get you there in the end. You need to die and be raised. You need, that is, to come out altogether from the 'worldly' sphere presided over by the 'elements of the world', the shadowy powers that operate within the present creation, doomed as it is to decay and perish. You need to belong instead to God's new world, the new creation that is being brought in to replace the old. The truly human life you seek – the life of a genuine, glad holiness that runs right through the personality – is to be found in that new world.

And the good news is that, if you belong to the Messiah, you already do belong to that new world. One of the main things Paul longs for new Christians to realize is *what is already true of them 'in Christ'*. Because the Messiah and his people are so closely bound up with one another, he lays it down as a basic principle: what is true of him is true of them. It may not feel like it. Learning to *believe* what doesn't at the moment *feel* true is an essential part of being a Christian, just as learning that I had to drive off in the opposite direction was an essential part of getting where I wanted to be. This is what the life of faith is all about.

And the key things that are true of the Messiah, which are already true of those 'in him' whether they feel it or not, are of course the two Paul highlights here: he died, and he was raised from the dead. The two paragraphs of this little section (which together look back to 2.12) make this quite clear. You died with the Messiah; so you don't belong in the old world any more, and regulations that are relevant there aren't relevant for you. You were raised with the Messiah; so you possess a true life in God's new world, the 'upper' or 'heavenly' world. That's where the real 'you' is now to be found.

This isn't a 'super-spiritual' world in the sense of a world which leaves the created order behind for ever. One day God will flood the present creation with the new life which is currently hidden in the heavenly realm. One day Jesus the Messiah, who cannot at the moment be seen within the old world, will appear again – when God transforms the whole cosmos so that what is at present unseen will become visible, and earth and heaven be joined for ever in the fulfilled new creation. And when that happens, all those who are 'in Christ', whose present true life is 'hidden with the king, in God', will appear as well, as the glorious renewed human beings they already really are.

Once you realize that, there appears before you the new way towards a genuine, fulfilling holiness. 'If you were raised to life with the king, search for the things that are above!' Learn to think about the things that are above, not the things that belong to the present world of change and decay. In fact, learning to *think*, rather than merely going with the flow of the world on the one hand, or blindly obeying what look like stringent regulations on the other, is part of the key to it all. One aspect of Christian maturity, and certainly one of the road signs on the surprising route to Christian holiness, is that the mind must grasp the truth: 'you died, and your life has been hidden with the king, in God!' Once the mind has grasped it, the heart and will may start to come on board. And once that happens the way lies open to joyful Christian holiness. Don't settle for short cuts.

THE NEW WAY OF LIFE

1 Peter 3.8–16

[8]The aim of this is for you all to be like-minded, sympathetic and loving to one another, tender-hearted and humble. [9]Don't repay evil for evil, or slander for slander, but rather say a blessing. This is what you were called to, so that you may inherit a blessing.

> [10]For the one who wants to love life and see good days
> should guard the tongue from evil, and the lips from
>   speaking deceit;
> [11]should turn away from evil and do good;
> should seek peace, and follow after it.
> [12]For the Lord's eyes are upon the righteous, and his ears
>   are open to their prayer,
> but the face of the Lord is against those who do evil.

[13]Who is there, then, to harm you if you are eager to do what is right? [14]But if you do suffer because of your righteous behaviour, God's blessing is upon you! 'Don't fear what they fear; don't be disturbed.' [15]Sanctify the Messiah as Lord in your hearts, and always be ready to make a reply to anyone who asks you to explain the hope that is in you. [16]Do it, though, with gentleness and respect. Hold on to a good conscience, so that when people revile your good behaviour in the Messiah they may be ashamed.

Most of us know the feeling of getting into a car we haven't driven before. You have a look round, see where the switch for the lights is, check the angle of the mirrors, and so on. It may take a moment to figure out, with some of today's cars, how to start the engine. But then, as you drive off, you revert to instinct. You think you're putting the lights on, and the windscreen wipers start up. Or the other way around. It's harder to change these little habits than we might think.

The same is true in relationships. A child, growing up, learns how to be a friend with the two or three children closest at hand. But then, perhaps when they move to a different school, there are different challenges. People don't respond in the same way. For a week or two the child may feel like a fish out of water. It may take an effort to work at doing things differently.

And so on through life. The point doesn't need to be stressed.

But it does need to be stressed when it's a matter of Christians learning to navigate in the dangerous new world they find themselves in. This was so in the first century, and it's increasingly so in the twenty-first. In what used to be thought of as the 'Christian' West, particularly Europe and North America, it used to be taken for granted that we lived in a 'Christian' country. In fact, unless people were obviously Jews, Muslims or some other definite religion, it was assumed that everyone was, more or less, 'Christian'. Now all that has been swept away, and anyone who really is 'Christian' may well stand out. In some quarters – politics, art, the media and particularly journalism – anyone known as a Christian may well attract scorn, criticism or even discrimination. In other words, Christians in the Western world are in a process of rejoining the mainstream. This is what it was like from the beginning. This is what it's like for probably a majority of Christians in the world today – in China, in many officially Muslim countries, and so on.

But it's not easy for Western Christians, faced with this shift, to unlearn old habits and learn the necessary new ones. We are not as used, as many Christians have had to be, to treading the fine line between sinking without trace into the surrounding culture, on the one hand, and adopting a stand-offish, holier-than-thou approach on the other. High-profile cases in the media, like an airline worker who was sacked for refusing to remove the cross she was wearing, have drawn our attention to this quite new set of circumstances. How does a Christian behave when surrounded by a world that doesn't understand what we think we're about, and is potentially hostile?

The answer comes in Peter's quotation from Psalm 34. *Seek peace, and follow after it*. It may be hard to find, this 'peace' which we're supposed to be looking for, but we should hunt it down as you would a favourite book that you can't put your hand on around the house. You should follow after it in the way you would a dog that has panicked and run off in a busy town. Don't expect 'peace' to come to you when you whistle. You have to do the work. You have to learn the new habit.

You have to learn it because it will be all too easy to lapse into the way many people behave. Here is the irony: Christians are supposed to stand out as distinctive, but when we do, and are mocked or criticized for it, we are tempted to mock and criticize right back – and then we are no longer distinctive, because we are behaving just like everyone else! Another victory for the hostile world: when Christians 'give as good as they get', repaying slander with slander, they are colluding with the surrounding world, just as surely as if they went along with immorality or financial corruption.

The new habits of heart and life are, then, to be learned in the comparatively safe environment of the church itself (verse 8), so that they can then be practised and applied in the wider world (verses 9 and 12–16). Sadly, it's all too easy to get this badly wrong, even in the church. But Peter, like Paul in one passage after another, insists on this as a basic rule of life: like-minded, sympathetic, loving, tender-hearted and humble. We may think of some people as naturally tender-hearted, and others as naturally a bit rough and cross-grained. But the early Christians assumed that they were all called to become tender-hearted, however difficult that might be. That's why we are given the holy spirit, to enable us to work at the new habits of heart and life.

I mentioned cars before, purely as an illustration. But of course the way we drive, and (not least) the things we think and say about other drivers, are major challenges for many of us. Here is that person dawdling along when we, stuck behind, are nearly late for an appointment! How dare they get in our way? And as we finally overtake, we are strongly tempted to look round at the person, sum up their character in a glance, and think ourselves vastly superior. We get away with it in the privacy of a car (as people do when contributing anonymously to blogs), but the corrosive effect on our character, our habits of mind and heart, is disastrous. It will emerge, if we're not very careful, in more public and shaming places.

The wisdom of Psalm 34, then, is all the more needed today: guard the tongue the way you would fence in an unbroken horse. Stop it doing damage. Then, and perhaps only then, you will be ready to face the hostile world, which may well attack even

when you are doing right, let alone when you are letting yourself down ('You Christians! You think you're so holy but actually
you're no better than the rest of us – in fact, probably
a lot worse.') Then and only then will you be able to 'make
a reply to anyone who asks you to explain the hope that is
in you' (verse 15). It must be done, as everything must be
done, with gentleness and respect, not implying that we are
terribly clever or superior because we've got this new religion
all figured out.

And, in particular, hold on to a good conscience. This is
vital. Day by day, hour by hour, we need to keep a watch over
our inner moral monitoring system. Don't let it get rusty.
Don't start ignoring it or telling it to be quiet. And this is not
for your own sake merely (though you are yourself at risk if
you try to silence your conscience). It is outward-looking.
A good Christian conscience means a good witness in a puzzled
and suspicious world. It may take time to have its effect, but
that's a lot better than a single moment of stupidity which gives
the watching world the perfect excuse to ignore the gospel ever
afterward.

BUILDING A CHRISTIAN CHARACTER

2 Peter 1.1–11

[1]Simon Peter, a slave and apostle of Jesus the Messiah, to those
who have obtained a share of faith equal to ours in the righteousness of our God and saviour Jesus the Messiah: [2]may grace and
peace be multiplied to you, in the knowledge of God and of
Jesus our Lord.

[3]God has bestowed upon us, through his divine power, everything that we need for life and godliness, through the knowledge
of him who called us by his own glory and virtue. [4]The result
is that he has given us, through these things, his precious
and wonderful promises; and the purpose of all this is so that
you may run away from the corruption of lust that is in the

world, and may become partakers of the divine nature. [5]So, because of this, you should strain every nerve to supplement your faith with virtue, and your virtue with knowledge, [6]and your knowledge with self-control, and your self-control with patience, and your patience with piety, [7]and your piety with family affection, and your family affection with love. [8]If you have these things in plentiful supply, you see, you will not be wasting your time, or failing to bear fruit, in relation to your knowledge of our Lord Jesus the Messiah. [9]Someone who doesn't have these things, in fact, is so short-sighted as to be actually blind, and has forgotten what it means to be cleansed from earlier sins. [10]So, my dear family, you must make the effort all the more to confirm that God has called you and chosen you. If you do this, you will never trip up. [11]That is how you will have, richly laid out before you, an entrance into the kingdom of God's coming age, the kingdom of our Lord and saviour Jesus the Messiah.

My grandson, aged one and a half, was taken the other day into a big toyshop. It was a riot of exciting things, all in bright colours. From floor to ceiling, from one end of the shop to the other, and all over the tables and stands in the middle, there were so many exciting things to see that he didn't know where to start. He looked quickly this way and that, then round, then up and down. He was in happy shock at this overload of delight. All he could say – one of his few words, but most expressive – was, 'WOW'.

That's a bit how I feel on reading quickly through the beginning of the letter we call 2 Peter. Every sentence, every word almost, glitters and flashes. Every idea beckons and says, 'Look at me! This is fascinating!' And it is. But if we are to make a start it will be good to see the big picture within which all this cluster of exciting and challenging ideas means what it means.

The big picture is *what God wants for his people*. All too often, people think that 'religion', or even 'Christian faith', is about what God wants *from* us – good behaviour, renunciation of things we like, a gritted-teeth morality of forcing ourselves to behave unnaturally. This is a total caricature. Here, in this breathtaking paragraph from verses 3 to 11, we see the truth.

First, God has already given us everything we need: a starter kit, if you like, for all that we need to become (verse 3). There is indeed quite a lot in this letter about the moral effort we have to make. But Peter is quite clear. It all comes from God in the first place.

Second, he wants nothing less for us than that we should come to share his own very nature (verse 4). Some Christians have felt uneasy about this idea, as though the humility to which we are so often exhorted ought to stop us short from thinking of actually sharing God's very being or nature. Others, though (particularly in the Eastern Christian traditions), have seen this as central to what it means to be a Christian. After all, if we say that the holy spirit is fully divine, and if we say that the holy spirit comes to live within us and transform us from within, what is that but to say that the divine nature is already dwelling within us, leading us forward until we are suffused with God's own presence and power? Obviously for most of us, most of the time, it won't feel like that. But that may be because we are not yet adept at recognizing what actually happens when God takes up residence in someone's life.

Third, God has indeed called and chosen those who find themselves following Jesus (verse 10). In this verse Peter urges his readers to 'confirm' this call and choice. He doesn't mean that they can make *God* more sure of it; rather, they can make themselves more sure. This leads directly to the fourth point: God has already set up his 'kingdom', his sovereign rule over earth as well as heaven (verse 11). When 'the age to come' has fully and finally those who in the present time follow Jesus will find that they are welcomed into that ultimate heaven-and-earth reality.

All this is just the outer framework for this remarkable passage, but it is all the more important because it shows that whatever *we* do by way of obedience and allegiance to God and the gospel, it all takes place within the grace of God, by means of the promise of God, through the power of God, and leading to the kingdom of God. That's a great place to start.

But it's not a good place to stop, because, as you will have noticed, the passage has plenty more besides. Central to it all is the idea that, by God's grace and power in our lives, we are to learn the discipline of Christian moral development. This has sometimes been frowned upon, as though it was, after all, 'me making myself good enough for God', and leading to pride or arrogance ('See what a fine Christian I've become!'). The framework I've just sketched should make it clear that nothing could be farther from the truth. But once this point is grasped, there are two basic things which must happen.

The first is that we must 'run away from the corruption of lust', in order to become partakers of God's own nature. Interesting, isn't it, that we are told to resist the devil (1 Peter 5.9), but, both here and in 2 Timothy 2.22, to run away from the lust which drags us down to the sub-human level. The word for 'run away from' is sometimes translated as 'shun', as though merely pushing these things away, like someone refusing a second helping of food, were enough, but neither Paul nor Peter is satisfied with that. Think of Joseph when Potiphar's wife tried to seduce him (Genesis 39). She made a grab at him, but he ran away. That isn't cowardice. A coward, as a wise old writer once put it, saves his prospects at the cost of his honour; Joseph did the opposite. Both Paul and Peter want us to do the same.

This running away from the lusts of the flesh isn't a negative thing, despite what people will rather frantically tell you today. Lust is a drug. Like all drugs it demands more and more but gives less and less. It turns people into shadows of real human beings. Like shady financial dealings, it 'corrupts': it does to the moral fibre what cancer does to physical cells.

Peter is urging his readers to go in the opposite direction. Become more fully human, he says, by building one aspect of Christian character on top of another: faith, virtue, knowledge, self-control, patience, piety, family affection, and finally love. All these take thought; all these take effort. They don't happen by accident. You have to want to do them; you have to choose to do them. But when you do, and pray for God's grace, promises and power to help, you will be coming to know Jesus the Messiah.

3

THE GREATEST OF THE VIRTUES

THE MOST IMPORTANT COMMANDMENT
Mark 12.28–34

[28]One of the legal experts came up, and overheard the discussion. Realizing that Jesus had given a splendid answer, he put a question of his own.

'Which commandment', he asked, 'is the first one of all?'

[29]'The first one', replied Jesus, 'is this: "Listen, Israel: the Lord your God, the Lord is one; [30]and you shall love the Lord your God with all your heart, and with all your soul, and with all your understanding, and with all your strength." [31]And this is the second one: "You shall love your neighbour as yourself." No other commandment is greater than these ones.'

[32]'Well said, Teacher,' answered the lawyer. 'You are right in saying that "he is one and there is no other beside him", [33]and that "to love him with all the heart, and with all the intelligence, and with all the strength" and "to love one's neighbour as oneself" is worth far more than all burnt offerings and sacrifices.'

[34]Jesus saw that his answer came out of deep understanding.

'You are not far from God's kingdom,' he said to him.

After that, nobody dared put any more questions to him.

If the house is on fire, what will you grab as you escape?

Your children, of course, if they can't walk themselves.

Your wallet. Your computer. Your passport and personal documents.

A precious photograph. The wristwatch your grandfather gave you. A stack of letters from someone you love dearly.

You look on from a safe distance as everything else is burnt to ashes. You realize the significance of what you've just done.

You have made some important choices. These things are more valuable to you than tables and chairs, china and glass, clothes, books, hi-tech equipment, and all the thousand other things that find a place in a home. You have discovered where your priorities really lie.

The question the lawyer asked Jesus was like that. Faced with the whole volume of Jewish law, which commandment really matters? Which one will you grasp on to in a moment of crisis? And what is the significance of that choice? What are you saying about the others?

This is about far more than 'how to construct a code of personal ethics', but let's take that aspect of it first. The Jewish law begins with worship, with the love of God, because if it's true that we're made in God's image we will find our fullest meaning, our true selves, the more we learn to love and worship the one we are designed to reflect. No half measures: heart, soul, mind and strength – that is, every aspect of human life – is to be poured out gladly in worship of the one true God. Whatever we do, we are to do for him. If we truly lived like that for a single day, God's kingdom would have come on earth as it is in heaven. And – this is the point – Jesus seems to think that through his kingdom-work this commandment is now within our reach.

Nor does Jesus stop there. The lawyer hasn't asked him about his second choice, but it's so important to his whole mission that he adds it anyway. 'Love your neighbour as yourself'; this doesn't mean loving others *instead of* ourselves, but showing to all people the same respect and care that we show to ourselves. Elsewhere in the gospel stories (e.g. Luke 10) this is developed and applied in more detail. Again, if people lived by this rule, most of the world's greatest problems would be solved over-night. Once more, Jesus implies that his kingdom-work will bring this commandment within reach. He really expects his followers to live it out, because he believes that God is now ful-filling his ancient promise to renew people's hearts. That's where writers like Paul take up the story.

Jesus' answer to the scribe's question carries another important implication. His 'first commandment' is a version of the central Jewish prayer, the *Shema* ('Shema' means 'listen', as in 'Listen, Israel . . .'). Devout Jews, from Jesus' day to our own, pray this prayer regularly every day. Jesus is claiming nothing less than this: that through his work, his teaching, and the things he has come to Jerusalem to achieve, the central prayer and hope of Judaism is being fulfilled. This isn't designed as a 'new religion', a way of life somehow different from what pious Jews sought after. This is the fulfilment of the law and the prophets.

But this in turn leads to the clear implication, which is hugely important for what Mark is telling us about Jesus in Jerusalem. The lawyer, musing on Jesus' answer, draws out a meaning which Jesus hadn't said out loud but which was certainly there. If these commandments are the primary ones, if this is what worshipping, loving and serving God is all about, then all that the Temple stands for, the daily, weekly and annual round of sacrifices and offerings, is virtually unnecessary. When a crisis comes, loving God and one's neighbour still matters; sacrifices don't.

The lawyer has grasped, and agreed with, Jesus' underlying meaning. No wonder Jesus commends him with the breathtaking words: 'You are not far from God's kingdom.'

At one level, then, this passage enables us to understand more fully what Jesus thought his work was all about, and how his overall mission was bound to challenge the centrality of the Temple – a highly controversial, not to say dangerous, thing to suggest. Jesus really did believe that through his kingdom-mission Israel's God would enable people to worship and love him, and to love one another, in a new way, the way promised in the prophets, the way that stemmed from renewed hearts and lives.

At another level, this comes as a considerable challenge to all contemporary Christians. Would anyone looking at us – our churches, our lives, the societies that claim in some sense to be 'Christian' – ever have guessed that the man we claim to follow saw his followers as being people like this? Or to put it another way: when the crisis comes, what remains solid in your life and the life of your community? Wholehearted love of God and neighbour? Or the mad scramble of everyone trying to save their own skins?

LOVE ONE ANOTHER

John 15.9–17

[9]'As the father loved me,' Jesus continued, 'so I loved you. Remain in my love. [10]If you keep my commands, you will remain in my love, just as I have kept my father's commands, and remain in his love. [11]I've said these things to you so that my joy may be in you, and so that your joy may be full.

[12]'This is my command: love one another, in the same way that I loved you. [13]No one has a love greater than this, to lay down your life for your friends. [14]You are my friends, if you do what I tell you. [15]I'm not calling you "servants" any longer; servants don't know what their master is doing. But I've called you "friends", because I've let you know everything I heard from my father.

[16]'You didn't choose me. I chose you, and I appointed you to go and bear fruit, fruit that would last. Then the father will give you whatever you ask in my name. [17]This is my command to you: love one another.'

Like an innocent child wandering by itself into a kitchen and pressing the switches that will set the house on fire, some biblical texts have been taken out of their original setting and used in ways that would have horrified the original speaker or writer. Here in this passage we have one with exactly that history.

'No one', said Jesus, 'has a love greater than this, to lay down your life for your friends' (verse 13). That is true, gloriously true.

Indeed, Jesus was on his way to his own execution as the most dramatic example of the point (see John 10.11; 13.1). The cross is clearly in view here, when Jesus says that laying down your life for your friends is the highest form of love, and then says 'and you, of course, are my friends' (verse 14). But during the First World War (1914–18), this text was used again and again, in sermons and lectures, set to music and sung by great choirs, with one single meaning: therefore *you*, young man – they were mostly young men – must go off to the front line, do what you're told and if necessary die for your country.

They did, in their tens of thousands. God honours, I believe, the self-sacrifice and dedication of those who sincerely and devoutly believed they were doing their duty. But I also believe God judges those who use texts like this as a convenient rhetorical trick to put moral pressure on other people, when what they needed was a bit of moral pressure on themselves to ask: Why are we doing this at all? If we must have a war, is this really the best way of fighting it? Are these 'sacrifices' (another convenient 'religious' word; people spoke of 'the final sacrifice', forgetting that in the Bible human sacrifice was condemned over and over again) the best way both of winning the war and of preparing ourselves for the world that will need rebuilding after it's all over?

The easy identification of 'our' side with God's side has been a major problem ever since Christianity became the official religion of the Roman state in the fourth century. Ironically, as Western Europe has become less and less Christian in terms of its practice, its leaders seem to have made this identification more and more, so that both sides in the major world wars of the twentieth century were staffed, as we have already noted, by Christian chaplains praying for victory.

This sits uneasily alongside a passage like this one, where the talk is of love, not war. In a world of danger and wickedness, it won't do for everyone to pretend there are no hard decisions to be made. But precisely one of the great dangers, and great wickednesses, of the world is the very common belief that fighting is a fine thing, that war is a useful way of settling disputes, and that, to put it crudely, might is right. One of the reasons human civilization has struggled to promote justice is the recognition that things aren't that easy. And justice, at its best, knows that it has only a negative function: to clear the decks and leave the world open for people to love one another.

You can't legislate for love; but God, through Jesus, can command you to love. Discovering the difference between what law cannot achieve and what God can and does achieve is one of the great arts of being human, and of being Christian. In the present passage we are brought in on the secret of it all.

The 'command' to love is given by one who has himself done everything that love can do. When a mother loves a child, she creates the context in which the child is free to love her in return. When a ruler really does love his or her subjects, and when this becomes clear by generous and warm-hearted actions, he or she creates a context in which the subjects can and will love them in return. The parody of this, seen with awesome clarity in George Orwell's book *Nineteen Eighty-Four*, is when the totalitarian ruler ('Big Brother'), who has done nothing but oppress and terrify his subjects, nevertheless orders them to love him. And the devastating climax, after the initially resisting subjects have been brainwashed, is that it works. At the end of the book, the hero is, in a sense, happy. 'He loved Big Brother.' And the reader knows that at this moment the hero has ceased to be truly human.

Jesus, though, issues the command that we are to love one another, and so to remain in his love, because he has acted out, and will act out, the greatest thing that love can do. He has come to make us more human, not less. He has come to give us freedom and joy (verse 11), not slavery and a semi-human stupor. He has come so that we can bear fruit that will last (verse 16), whether in terms of a single life changed because we loved somebody as Jesus loved us, or in terms of a single decision that we had to take, a single task we had to perform, through which, though we couldn't see it at the time, the world became a different place. Love makes both the lover and the beloved more truly human.

At the heart of it all is the humility that comes from knowing who's in charge. 'You didn't choose me. I chose you' (verse 16). I was once asked, on the radio, which religion I would choose if I could. I pointed out that the idea of 'choosing your religion' was a mistake in the first place. Religions are not items on the supermarket shelf that we can pick and choose – though many today try to run their lives that way. Or, if they are, you'd have to say that following Jesus wasn't a 'religion'. It is a personal relationship of love and loyalty to the one who has loved us more than we can begin to imagine. And the test of that love and loyalty remains the simple, profound, dangerous and difficult command: love one another.

THE CHARACTER OF LOVE

1 Corinthians 13.1–7

> [1]If I speak in human languages, or even
> in those of angels, but do not have love,
> then I've become a clanging gong or else
> a clashing cymbal. [2]And if I should have
> prophetic gifts, and know all mysteries,
> all knowledge, too; have faith, to move the mountains,
> but have no love – I'm nothing. [3]If I give
> all my possessions to the poor, and, for pride's sake,
> my very body, but do not have love,
> it's useless to me.
>
> [4]Love's great-hearted; love is kind,
> knows no jealousy, makes no fuss,
> is not puffed up, [5]no shameless ways,
> doesn't force its rightful claim,
> doesn't rage or bear a grudge,

[6]doesn't cheer at others' harm,
rejoices, rather, in the truth.
[7]Love bears all things, believes all things,
love hopes all things, endures all things.

When people say, as they sometimes do, that Paul must have been a very difficult person to have around – that he seems to have been awkward, cantankerous, argumentative, and generally an unpleasant character – this passage is one I often quote in reply.

It seems to me impossible to imagine that this passage could have been written in a very personal letter by the founder of a community, to that community, *unless he knew, and he knew that they knew, that this is the kind of person he himself was.* Of course, that doesn't mean that Paul lived up to this stunning picture of love every minute of every day. But that he had (unlike some of the teachers in Corinth) spent his life and energy being what he was and doing what he was for the sake of other people, copying and embodying the love that Jesus himself had shown in dying on the cross, I think we can be sure.

The very word 'love' causes us all sorts of problems in the English language. Our vocabulary has become impoverished. Where Greek has four words, we have at most two – 'love' and 'affection'. All right, there are related ones like 'fondness' and 'compassion', but they none of them come near what Paul is talking about. The older word 'charity' has come to be associated so closely with the splendid work of organizing and administering relief for those in need that it has ceased to be useful as a translation here.

The description Paul gives in verses 4–7 is not an account of what Hollywood means by 'love'. Romantic or erotic love, at its best, is like a signpost to the thing Paul is talking about: when two people are 'in love', they often make promises which sound like verses 4–7, but the emotional and physical energy which gets them that far won't get them all the way to fulfilling the promises. It takes a commitment of mind and will – which often then, to its own surprise, brings erotic love along with it.

Nor is what Paul is talking about the same thing as we mean when we say 'I love tennis', or 'I love the colour orange'. But if we love tennis, or a colour, as much as that, we may again take the first steps of mind and will to do things which will enable us to play, or watch, more tennis, or to paint, or observe, our favourite colour.

No: what Paul has in mind is something which, though like our other loves in some ways, goes as far beyond them as sunlight goes beyond candles or electric light. Look closely for a moment at the type of person he describes in verses 4–7. This passage describes someone doing and being things which in the eyes of the world would be rubbish. The newspapers are full of the opposite every day; and most people, in ordering their own lives, assume a set of values in which what Paul is urging is at best a noble but far-off ideal.

Paul begins by insisting that it is love that gives meaning and appropriate flavour to all other Christian living. He stacks up all the impressive things that the Corinthians might do (he says 'though *I* do these things', but the assumption is that he's talking about them), and asserts firmly that none of them are of any advantage unless there is love as well. Verse 1 declares that, without love, speaking in tongues and languages of any and every kind is simply a way of making a loud but incomprehensible noise. Verse 2 lists several of the other 'gifts' that Paul mentioned in chapter 12 and will return to in chapter 14; this time he says that without love someone who does all these things will be 'nothing' – not even a noisy gong. Verse 3 imagines someone taking one of Jesus' commands to its literal extreme, giving away all one's possessions (Mark 10.21), perhaps in order to feed the poor (the same verb can mean something like that). Paul then imagines himself handing over his body, perhaps to be tortured or to death, in order to be able, like the martyrs of old, to feel that he really had something to boast of. (Some manuscripts say 'to be burnt', which in Paul's language is a very similar word to 'boast'.) But even accomplishments like these, in the absence of love, 'won't do me any good at all'. As we have often seen, Paul clearly imagines that on the last day those who have been justified by faith in the present will be judged according to the life they have lived (see, for instance, 1 Corinthians 3.10–15); and the one thing that will count above all else on that day is love.

But what then does he mean by 'love'? Verses 4–7, the heart of the poem, describe it. Line by line of the description is clear in itself. Perhaps the best thing to do with a passage like this is to take it slowly, a line at a time, and to reflect on at least three things: first, ways in which we see this quality in Jesus himself; second, ways in which we see it (or more likely, alas, don't see it) in ourselves; and third, ways in which, if we were like that, it would work out in practice.

Such an exercise should never be undertaken simply in order to feel either good about oneself or frustrated at one's lack of moral growth. It should always be done in prayer; and at the third stage, as we ask for grace to envisage situations where we could behave differently, we should try to imagine what doing that would feel like, what steps we would have to take to make it happen, to avoid lapsing back into our normal behaviour. Then, when we're faced with the relevant situation, we will at least have a choice which we have already thought about, instead of behaving as creatures of habit. And of course the ultimate aim is for *this* way of life, peculiar though it seems and almost unbelievable at points, to become the engrained way we habitually behave. Some people have taken steps along that road ahead of us. When we meet them it's like hearing gentle music, or seeing a beautiful sunrise. But this life is within reach of each one of us; because it is the life of Jesus, the life inspired by the spirit, the life which is our birthright within the Messiah's body.

What's more, as Paul insists – and this is the point of him saying all this here in the letter – this is the life which will bring the right sort of order to the chaos of faction-fighting and spiritual jealousy within the church. This poem serves a purpose, and in enjoying it and trying to make it our own we should have an eye on the equivalent purpose in our lives, and our churches, as well.

GOD IS LOVE

1 John 4.7–21

[7]Beloved, let us love one another, because love is from God, and all who love are fathered by God and know God. [8]The one who does not love has not known God, because God is love. [9]This is how God's love has appeared among us: God sent his only son into the world, so that we should live through him. [10]Love consists in this: not that we loved God, but that he loved us and sent his son to be the sacrifice that would atone for our sins. [11]Beloved, if that's how God loved us, we ought to love one another in the same way. [12]Nobody has ever seen God. If we love one another, God abides in us and his love is completed in us. [13]That is how we know that we abide in him, and he in us, because he has given us a portion of his spirit. [14]And we have seen and bear witness that the father sent the son to be the world's saviour. [15]Anyone who confesses that Jesus is God's son, God abides in them and they abide in God. [16]And we have known and have believed the love which God has for us.

God is love; those who abide in love abide in God, and God abides in them. [17]This is what makes love complete for us, so that we may have boldness and confidence on the day of judgment, because just as he is, so are we within this world. [18]There is no fear in love; complete love drives out fear. Fear has to do with punishment, and anyone who is afraid has not been completed in love. [19]We love, because he first loved us. [20]If someone says, 'I love God', but hates their brother

> or sister, that person is a liar. Someone who doesn't love a brother or sister whom they have seen, how can they love God, whom they haven't seen? [21]This is the command we have from him: anyone who loves God should love their brother or sister too.

Statistics aren't everything, but sometimes they are quite revealing. The word 'love', or some form of it, occurs no fewer than twenty-seven times in these fifteen verses. No need to ask, then what the subject-matter is here. 'Love' is what John has on his mind.

The vital connection of thought here goes like this. John has just stressed that Jesus, the Messiah, has indeed come in the flesh, and that to deny that is to reveal oneself as a false prophet. But this is no mere dogmatic shibboleth, a meaningless formula which people have to learn in order to pass some arbitrary doctrinal test. It is a symptom of what Christianity is all about. The Christian faith grows directly out of, and must directly express, the belief that in Jesus the Messiah the one true God has revealed himself to be – love incarnate. And those who hold this faith, and embrace it as the means of their own hope and life, must themselves reveal the self-same fact before the watching world. Love incarnate must be the badge that the Christian community wears, the sign not only of who they are but of who their God is.

How easy to write, how hard to achieve. Only today I was talking to someone who, commenting gloomily on various experiences of actual church life, suggested that churches should have a 'danger' sign outside, warning people to expect nasty, gossipy, snide conversation and behaviour if they came in. That, sadly, has always been a reality in church life. That is why, from St Paul onwards, Christian writers have been at pains to insist that it should not be like that with us. The rule of love is not an optional extra. It is of the very essence of what we are about. If this means we need some new reformations, so be it.

Follow the argument through. Basic to it all, in verses 7–10, is the fact that God's love is revealed precisely in sending Jesus, his son, into the world to be the sacrifice that would atone for our sins. Standing at the foot of the cross, gazing on the length to which God's love has gone for us, it's impossible (unless we are particularly hard-hearted; unless, as he says, we simply haven't known God at all) not to sense the power and possibilities within that love. This is the force that has changed the world, and could still change the world if only the followers of Jesus would really come on board with it.

Therefore, 'if that's how God loved us, we ought to love one another in the same way' (verse 11). This is, if anything, an even stronger statement than many might imagine. You could hear it as simply saying, 'There: God has set us an example; we should copy it.' That is true. But the next verse shows a greater depth. 'Nobody has ever seen God. If we love one another, God abides in us and his love is completed in us.'

To get the point, stand that statement in parallel with the concluding verse (1.18) in the majestic Prologue to St John's gospel: 'Nobody has ever seen God. The only-begotten God, who is intimately close to the father – he has brought him to light.' The meaning of that statement is striking: we don't really know who 'God' is – until we look at Jesus. Now we see the meaning of our present statement in 1 John 4.12: people don't really know who 'God' is – until they see it revealed in the life of Christians. Until, that is, 'his love is completed in us'. What God launched decisively in Jesus, he wants to complete in and through us. As Jesus unveiled God before a surprised and unready world, so must we. Love is that important.

All this can and must come about because of the gift of God's spirit. The spirit enables us to bear witness to what the father has done in sending the son. Again, the witness must of course come not in word but in deed, as John says (1 John 3.18). Our love must 'come in the flesh', just as God's love did.

That's why, at the end of this passage, John comes back to the same point. If you say you love God, but don't love your brother or sister (he means a fellow member of the Christian community), you are quite simply telling lies. The same door that opens to let out your love to God is the door that opens to let out love to your neighbour. If you're not doing the latter, you're not doing the former. It's as simple – and as devastating – as that.

We may well find this daunting. Who can live up to it? But in verses 17 and 18 John moves into almost lyrical mode as he talks not about the fear that we should have of being found out, of failing to come up to the mark, but of the boldness and confidence that we shall have on the day of judgment. He does not say, as we might expect, that we have this boldness and confidence because we look away from ourselves and simply trust in God's all-powerful, all-conquering love. No. He says that 'just as he is, so are we within this world'. What does he mean? He means, it seems, that if God revealed himself in the world by turning his love into flesh and blood, when we do the same we should realize that we are 'completing' God's love. What will be operating through us will be the true love of the true God.

When that happens, there is no need to fear any longer. Love that has been made complete in this way leaves no room for fear. Once you learn to give yourself to others as God gave himself to us, there is nothing to be afraid of any more, just a completed circle of love. No doubt this, like some other things John says, leaves us breathless, wondering if we will ever attain to that simplicity of faith and life. But did we expect that having the true, living God come to make his dwelling with us, inviting us to make our dwelling with him (verse 16), would be a kind of easy-going, half-hearted, hobby-religion? God has taken us utterly seriously. How can we not do the same with him?

At the heart of this passage we find, repeated, a little word which means a whole world to John, as in his gospel it means so much to Jesus himself. 'Those who *abide* in love *abide* in God, and God *abides* in them' (verse 16). This comes in various other places, including the previous verse, but this is its fullest expression. The word is a simple one, meaning 'dwell' or 'remain' or 'make one's home'; but the reality is profound, going to the heart of what Christian faith is all about. This is the meaning of the 'fellowship', the sharing of a common life, between the father, the son and all those who belong to the son, who confess 'that Jesus is God's son' (verse 15). It is a mutual indwelling: we in God and God in us. Once more, this is easy to say, but huge and hard to take in. Harder still to keep your balance, to maintain this life, day by day and year by year, with the dangerous winds of false prophecy blowing around our heads and the pull and drag of 'the world' at our feet. Only powerful love can keep us upright. And that powerful love is to be found, as always, as we gaze at the cross (verses 9–11).

4

THE PATH OF THE DISCIPLE

DO NOT WORRY
Matthew 6.25–34

[25]'So let me tell you: don't worry about your life – what to eat, what to drink; don't worry about your body – what to wear. There's more to life than food! There's more to the body than a suit of clothes! [26]Have a good look at the birds in the sky. They don't plant seeds, they don't bring in the harvest, they don't store things in barns – and your father in heaven feeds them! Think how different you are to them! [27]Can any of you add fifteen inches to your height just by worrying about it?

[28]'And why worry about what to wear? Take a tip from the lilies in the countryside. They don't work; they don't weave; [29]but, let me tell you, not even Solomon in all his finery was dressed as well as one of these. [30]So if God gives that sort of clothing even to the grass in the field, which is here today and on the bonfire tomorrow, isn't he going to clothe you too, you little-faith lot?

[31]'So don't worry away with your "What'll we eat?" and "What'll we drink?" and "What'll we wear?" [32]Those are all the kinds of things the Gentiles fuss about, and your heavenly father knows you need them all. [33]Instead, make your top priority God's kingdom and his way of life, and all these things will be given to you as well.

[34]'So don't worry about tomorrow. Tomorrow can worry about itself. One day's trouble at a time is quite enough.'

Has it ever struck you what a basically *happy* person Jesus was?

Oh yes, we know that, according to the prophecies, he was 'a man of sorrow, and acquainted with grief'. We know that the darkness and sadness of all the world descended on him as he went to the cross. The scene in Gethsemane, where he is wrestling with his father's will, and in agony wondering if he's come the right way, is one of the most harrowing stories ever told. We know that he wept at the tomb of Lazarus, and that he was sad when people refused to trust God and see the wonderful things he was doing.

But these are the exceptions, the dark patches painted on to the bright background. As we read a passage like this, we should see that it flows straight out of Jesus' own experience of life. He had watched the birds wheeling around, high up on the currents of air in the Galilean hills, simply enjoying being alive. He had figured out that they never seemed to do the sort of work that humans did, and yet they mostly stayed alive and well. He had watched a thousand different kinds of flowers growing in the fertile Galilee soil – the word translated 'lily' here includes several different plants, such as the autumn crocus, the anemone and the gladiolus – and had held his breath at their fragile beauty. One sweep of a scythe, one passing donkey, and this wonderful object, worth putting in an art gallery, is gone. Where did its beauty come from? It didn't spend hours in front of the mirror putting on make-up. It didn't go shopping in the market for fine clothes. It was just itself: glorious, God-given, beautiful.

Jesus had a strong, lively sense of the goodness of his father, the creator of the world. His whole spirituality is many a mile from those teachers who insisted that the present world was a place of shadows, gloom and vanity, and that true philosophy consisted in escaping it and concentrating on the things of the mind. His teaching grew out of his own experience. When he told his followers not to worry about tomorrow, we must assume he led them by example. He wasn't always looking ahead anxiously, making the present moment count only because of what might come next. No: he seems to have had the skill of living totally in the present, giving attention totally to the present task, celebrating the goodness of God here and now. If that's not a recipe for happiness, I don't know what is.

And he wanted his followers to be the same. When he urged them to make God their priority, it's important to realize which God he's talking about. He's not talking about a god who is distant from the world, who doesn't care about beauty and life and food and clothes. He's talking about the creator himself, who has filled the world with wonderful and mysterious things, full of beauty and energy and excitement, and who wants his human creatures above all to trust him and love him and receive their own beauty, energy and excitement from him.

So when Jesus tells us not to worry about what to eat, or drink, or wear, he doesn't mean that these things don't matter. He doesn't mean that we should prefer (as some teachers have suggested) to eat and drink as little as possible, and to wear the most ragged and disreputable clothes, just to show that we despise such things. Far from it! Jesus liked a party as much as anyone, and when he died the soldiers so admired his tunic that they threw dice for it rather than tearing it up. But the point was again priorities. Put the world first, and you'll find it gets moth-eaten in your hands. Put God first, and you'll get the world thrown in.

Nor does Jesus mean, of course, that we should not plant seeds and reap harvests, or that we should not work at weaving and spinning to make clothes. Rather, we should do these things with joy, because our God, our father, is the creator of all and wants to feed and clothe us – not gloomily, as though God were a mean tyrant who was out to get us and make life difficult for us.

Living totally without worry sounds, to many people, as impossible as living totally without breathing. Some people are so hooked on worry that if they haven't got anything to worry about they worry that they've forgotten something. Here, at the heart of the Sermon on the Mount, is an invitation that surprisingly few people even try to take up. Why not learn how to share the happiness of Jesus himself?

THE WISE AND WICKED SLAVES
Matthew 24.45–51

[45]'So,' Jesus went on, 'who then is the trustworthy and sensible slave, the one the master will set over his household, so that he will give them their meals at the right time? [46]Blessings on the servant whom the master, when he comes, finds doing just that. [47]I'm telling you the truth: he'll promote him to be over all his belongings. [48]But if the wicked slave says in his heart, "My master's taking his time", [49]and starts to beat the other slaves, and to feast and drink with the drunkards, [50]the master of that slave will come on a day he doesn't expect, and at a time he doesn't know. [51]He will cut him in two, and put him along with the hypocrites, where people will weep and grind their teeth.'

The managing director was returning from a meeting out of town, when he saw a familiar but unexpected sight. There, turning out of a street ahead of him, was one of his own company's vans. What was it doing here? The company didn't do business with anyone in this part of the town. What was going on?

He took the number of the van, and later in the day called the driver in. He confessed. He'd been moonlighting – working for another company at the same time, while he was supposed to be making deliveries for the company which owned the vans. He'd been, in that sense, a hypocrite, a play-actor, pretending to be one thing while in fact being another. That was his last day working for that company.

Of course, today they put electronic components into trucks and vans which record everything that happens – speed, rest periods, fuel consumption, you name it. 'The spy in the cab', the drivers call them, resentfully. But at least they know they aren't going to get away with cheating. No chance of the boss suddenly coming upon them doing something they shouldn't.

The scene changes, but the underlying drama is the same. Imagine a householder going away on business and coming back suddenly: will he find the workers (in Jesus' world, the slaves) doing what they should, or not? In that world a story about a master and servants would almost certainly be understood as a story about God and Israel. God has left Israel with tasks to perform; when he comes back, what will his verdict be on how they have accomplished them?

At the same time, there may be here a further twist to this plot, from the point of view of Jesus speaking to the disciples on the Mount of Olives. He is going to leave them with work to do: the gospel must be announced to all the nations (24.14). Some of them will have responsibilities within the young and struggling Christian community. How will they discharge them?

The options presented here are stark. The slave in charge of the household has duties, and must do them. If he thinks to himself that his master won't be back for a long while yet, and decides to live it up, have a good time, and (for good measure) ill-treat his fellow-slaves, he will be in deep trouble. He will be a play-actor, a hypocrite. He will be pretending to be one thing while being another.

The difference between the two types of slave – the one who kept watch and did what he should, and the one who forgot what he was about and did the opposite – isn't just the difference between good and bad, between obedience and disobedience. It's the difference between wisdom and folly.

It's worth taking a minute to notice where this either/or comes from. Deep within ancient Jewish tradition we find the book of Proverbs. There, mostly in short sayings but sometimes in more extended pictures, we find in a wealth of detail the contrast between the wise person and the foolish person. Of course, ultimately the wise person is the one who respects and honours God, and the fool is the one who forgets him. But their wisdom and folly work themselves out in a thousand different ways in daily life, in business, in the home and village, in making plans for the future, in how they treat other people, in their honesty or dishonesty, in their hard work or laziness, in their ability to recognize and avoid temptations to immorality. Jesus is here invoking this whole tradition of wisdom-writing, which continued to develop in Judaism after the Old Testament, and which came into early Christianity in books like the letter of James.

But now the point of 'wisdom' and 'folly' is not just being able to do what God wants in any and every situation. If the living God might knock at the door at any time, wisdom means being ready at any time. What's more, once Jesus has come, bringing God's kingdom to bear on the world, being wise or being foolish means knowing, or not knowing, what time it is in God's timetable. Wisdom consists not least, now, in realizing that the world has turned a corner with the coming of Jesus and that we must always be ready to give an account of ourselves.

Of course these warnings are held within the larger picture of the gospel, in which Jesus embodies the love of God which goes out freely to all and sundry. Of course we shall fail. Of course there will be times when we shall go to sleep on the job. Part of being a follower of Jesus is not that we always get everything right, but that, like Peter among others, we quickly discover where we are going wrong, and take steps to put it right.

But along with the welcome for sinners which Jesus announces, and the ready forgiveness that is always on offer when we fail and then come to our senses, there is the hard and high call to watchfulness and loyalty. You can't use God's grace as an excuse for going slack ('God will forgive me,' said one philosopher, 'that's his job'). Even when we don't think we're being watched, we can never forget that much is expected of those to whom much is given.

THE WISE AND FOOLISH GIRLS

Matthew 25.1–13

[1]'Then,' continued Jesus, 'the kingdom of heaven will be like ten girls who each took their own torches and went out to meet the bridegroom. [2]Five of them were silly, and five were sensible. [3]The silly ones took their torches, but didn't take oil with them. [4]The sensible ones took oil, in flasks, along with their torches.

[5]'The bridegroom took his time coming, and they all nodded off and went to sleep. [6]In the middle of the night a shout went up: "Here's the bridegroom! Come on and meet him!" [7]Then all the girls got up and trimmed the wicks of their torches.

[8]'The silly ones said to the sensible ones, "Give us some of your oil! Our torches are going out!"

[9]'But the sensible ones answered, "No! If we do that, there won't be enough for all of us together! You'd better go to the dealers and buy some for yourselves."

[10]'So off they went to buy oil. But, while they were gone, the bridegroom arrived. The ones who were ready went in with him to the wedding party, and the door was shut.

[11]'Later on the other girls came back. "Master, master!" they said, "open the door for us!"

[12]'"I'm telling you the truth," he said, "I don't know you."

[13]'So keep awake! You don't know the day or the hour.'

The guests had all arrived and were seated. The organ was playing. The bridegroom and the best man had been there half an hour in advance. The photographers were waiting. The flowers had all been beautifully arranged. The choir had practised their anthems. And the bride was nowhere to be seen.

Since I was supposed to be performing the service that day I went out of the church, and round the corner on to the street. Then I saw her. Her car was stuck in traffic a few hundred yards away. Eventually she and her bridesmaids had decided to walk. They were coming down the street. I stepped out into the road, in my full clerical robes, and held up the traffic. Cars hooted their horns. People waved and shouted 'good luck'. And we began the service a full fifteen minutes late.

Every culture has its own way of celebrating a wedding – and its own risks of getting things wrong. I once knew a family where people were so afraid of a car breaking down on the way to the church that they hired a second one to drive behind the first, empty, just in case. But in different cultures the risks will be different. In the Middle East to this day there are all sorts of traditional customs for what is after all one of the most important transitional moments in human life, when two people leave the security of their respective families and publicly declare that they are going to begin to live as a new, different family.

In the Middle East to this day there are some places where the customs at a wedding are quite similar to the ones described here. In the modern West, people don't normally get married in the middle of the night! But in that culture torchlight processions, late in the evening, are certainly known, and it seems as though the proceedings might have several stages, with the bridegroom likely to be delayed at an earlier venue before he arrives for the banquet itself, to be greeted at last by the bridesmaids.

So much for the local colour of this story, which otherwise might be confusing for people used to other customs. What else is going on here?

Even more obviously than the previous one, this story is rooted in the Jewish tradition of contrasting wisdom and folly – being sensible or being silly. The writer of Proverbs treats Wisdom and Folly as two women, and describes them calling out to men going by, and offering them their respective lifestyles. Now, in this story, Lady Wisdom and Mistress Folly have each become five young girls, and the story invites its hearers to decide which they'd rather be. Obviously, wisdom in this case means being ready with the oil for the lamp, and folly means not thinking about it until it's too late.

It's probably wrong to try to guess what the oil in the story 'stands for' (some have suggested that it means good works; others faith, or love, or almost any of the Christian virtues). It isn't that kind of story. Within the world of the story itself, it simply means being ready for the key moment. You can't squash all these parables together and make the details fit with each other; *all* the girls in this parable, including the 'wise' ones, go to sleep in verse 5, whereas in verse 13 Jesus tells his followers to stay awake. Again, that kind of detailed question misses the point. What matters is being ready; being prepared; being wise; thinking ahead, realizing that a crisis is coming sooner or later and that if you don't make preparations now, and keep them in good shape in the meantime, you'll wish you had.

WHERE TWO ROADS LEAD

Romans 6.20–23

> [20]When you were slaves of sin, you see, you were free in respect of covenant justice. [21]What fruit did you ever have from the things of which you are now ashamed? Their destination is death. [22]But now that you have been set free from sin and enslaved to God, you have fruit for holiness. Its destination is the life of the age to come. [23]The wages paid by sin, you see, are death; but God's free gift is the life of the age to come, in the Messiah, Jesus our Lord.

One of the things you have to learn when you move house is which roads lead where. I was Christmas shopping the other day in the new town where we have just settled, and as I drove out of a car park I saw a long queue of cars backed up down the main road. Eager to get home, I saw a side street which led, so it seemed, across town in the direction I wanted to go. I took it, only to discover it led into a cul-de-sac. Ah, but there was a small street leading off at the very bottom. I took that. It turned out to be a loop, bringing me back where I'd started.

It could have been worse. I once took what looked like a promising country lane, only to find myself getting stuck, miles out in the country, in a stream that had burst its banks and washed away part of the road surface. I have sometimes been tempted to ignore 'Danger' signs when driving near military ranges, and to take what would otherwise be the obvious route across the moors. And of course one can imagine situations worse again, such as trying to beat the traffic by driving through a line of road cones, only to discover that the bridge you find yourself on hasn't been finished yet and you are about to drive off the end and fall into the river.

The point is obvious, but when it comes to Christian ethics it is often missed. The rules and guidelines for Christian living are not there because God happens to like squashing people into a particular shape whether or not it's good for them, whether or not it will make them happy. The rules are there because they are the rules of the road, and it matters which road you take. One road will ultimately lead you not just into a cul-de-sac but into disaster. The other road leads you to life, life in a new dimension, life in all its fullness.

This, too, is easy to misunderstand. People have often supposed that the threat of ultimate death, and the promise of ultimate life, work simply on the principle of the carrot and the stick. God, on this model, treats us like ignorant donkeys, waving carrots over our noses ('Eternal life! How about that! Now then, get a move on!'), or, if we seem reluctant, giving us a swish with his stick ('You'll feel ashamed! You'll die! Don't do it!'). Maybe it does feel like that sometimes, but, if so, it's probably because we are looking at it wrongly. The point is quite different. Certain behaviour is, in its own character, destructive both to those who practise it and to those whose lives are affected all around. If (to take an obvious example) people regularly get drunk and go around smashing things up, they are damaging themselves and the world around. It isn't so much that some arbitrary standard declares that such behaviour is wrong and deserves punishment. Such behaviour already shows the signs of its destination. It has the smell of death already upon it. The ultimate punishment is not arbitrary, like putting someone into prison for failing to pay a tax bill. It is much more like what happens when someone drives recklessly over a cliff and falls to their death.

Conversely, when people behave in the patterns set out in the gospel and the early Christian teaching, there are signs of life already at work. The life of the age to come is not an arbitrary reward, like someone being given a medal for rescuing a child from drowning. It is much more like the reward that a father receives when the child he has rescued is his own beloved daughter.

Pause for a moment and examine that phrase, 'the life of the age to come'. It is often translated 'eternal life', and it clearly sums up Paul's view of the ultimate destination of God's people. But it is often misunderstood. Many people bring to the New Testament an assumed view of the final destination, 'heaven'. They think of sitting on clouds playing harps, perhaps; and though they perhaps know that's only a picture they still think of the reality in terms of an existence outside space, time and matter. But that is certainly not the New Testament picture, and it's certainly not Paul's idea of the ultimate destination. As a good first-century Jew – and his Christian theology has not changed this view, only deepened it and filled it out – he believed that there were two 'ages': the 'present age' and the 'age to come'. The present age (see, for instance, Galatians 1.4) was a time when wickedness continued to rule God's world. In the age to come, God's rule would triumph at last. The achievement of Jesus the Messiah had brought this 'age to come' forwards into the middle of the present age. Christians were summoned to live in the present in the light of that future, that future which had come to meet them in Jesus.

The future, though, remains God's gift (verse 23). Paul is careful to keep his balance. When you sin, you earn a wage, and the wage is death. But when you live according to God's way of holiness, you do not *earn* the life of the coming age. It remains a free gift, far greater than anything we could have deserved. Final judgment will be in accordance with the life we have led (2.1–16). But it will be 'in accordance with' in the same way that a symphony orchestra playing Beethoven at full blast is 'in accordance with' my feeble attempts to whistle the tune.

Romans 6 is a bracing chapter, one that the church desperately needs to listen to in our own day. It does not give us specific ethical instructions; for those, we must look elsewhere. It gives us the framework for thinking about why Christian behaviour matters, and how to put it into practice. People still assume, inside the churches as well as outside, that Christianity is simply a matter of a few strange and restrictive moral rules coupled with a few strange and outdated beliefs and practices. Even a few lines of Paul will put that nonsense to rest, and get us back on track for the serious and necessary business of genuine Christian holiness.

CHASING ON TO THE FINISH
Philippians 3.12–16

[12]I'm not implying that I've already received 'resurrection', or that I've already become complete and mature! No; I'm hurrying on, eager to overtake it, because King Jesus has overtaken me. [13]My dear family, I don't reckon that I have yet overtaken it. But this is my one aim: to forget everything that's behind, and to strain every nerve to go after what's ahead. [14]I mean to chase on towards the finishing post, where the prize waiting for me is the upward call of God in King Jesus.
[15]Those of us who are mature should think like this! If you think differently about it, God will reveal this to you as well. [16]Only let's be sure to keep in line with the position we have reached.

The athletics match had reached a critical stage. One of the final races was left to be run: the 440 yards (the old version of today's 400 metres). The athletes were bunched together as they came to the first bend, and one of them was pushed over and fell right off the track. Quick as a flash he was back on his feet, and, as though electrically charged by the incident, caught the other runners with a few paces to go and overtook them to win on the line. It was a famous victory, which features now in the movie *Chariots of Fire*.

What would you have done? Most of us, I suspect, would have accepted from the moment we fell over that we were out of the race, with no hope left. We might have been angry, but there would be nothing we could do about it. What had in fact just happened would keep us enslaved, with no hope of going on to what *might* have happened. With the athlete in question – the famous Eric Liddell – it was just the opposite. It was as though he had been reading this passage of Paul: forget what's behind, strain every nerve to go after what's ahead, and chase on towards the finishing post.

Paul ended the previous paragraph with talk of the resurrection which lies still in the future, and towards which, therefore, all Christians are drawn like athletes sprinting towards the end of the race. As he stresses in verse 13, it's important to concentrate on the one aim in view: keeping on going forwards towards that goal.

But in using his own path of discipleship as an example for the Philippian church to follow he wants to head off any idea that once you have become a mature Christian you have, as it were, 'arrived', in the sense that there is no more travelling to do. He is gently warning against any tendency to a super-spiritual view of Christianity which imagines that the full life of the age to come can be had in the present, without waiting for the resurrection itself.

Paul is quite clear about this. He hasn't 'arrived' in that sense, and nor has anyone else. True maturity, he insists, actually means knowing that you haven't arrived, and that you must still keep pressing on forwards towards the goal. The seasoned athlete knows that the race isn't won and lost until the end has been reached. To imagine that because you find yourself out in front of the pack you can slack off and take it easy, having 'arrived', would be disastrous. As he says in verse 16, it's important to maintain the position you've reached.

What then is the goal, the finishing line? Paul describes it in verse 14 with an interesting phrase: the prize that is waiting there, like a silver cup or medal for the winning athlete, is 'the upward call of God in King Jesus'. This has often been seen as simply 'heaven', the place 'up there' where Christians aim to go at the end.

But this can't be what Paul means. In verses 20 and 21 of this chapter he speaks not of our going up to heaven, but of the Lord, King Jesus himself, coming *from* heaven to earth, in order to transform the world and change our bodies so that they are like his own resurrected and glorified body. Living in 'heaven' isn't the goal we are aiming at; rather, it's living in God's new world with our new bodies. So the 'upward call' seems to be the resurrection life itself. Straining forwards towards it, like an athlete aiming at the finishing line and the prize that waits beyond it, means living in the present in the light of that future. (This is very close, in fact, to what Paul says a bit more fully in Colossians 3.1–4.)

None of this means, though, that Paul sees the Christian life as a gloomy struggle. Look again at verse 12. He is eager to 'overtake it' because the Messiah, Jesus, has 'overtaken him'. It's difficult to find one English word here that really catches the double meaning he wants. When he's talking about what he, Paul, still has to do, the word means 'to catch up', or 'to grasp the prize', or 'to attain the goal'. When he's talking about what Jesus has done to and for him, the word means 'has laid hold of me', 'has grasped me and taken control of me'. But it's the same word, and that's the point. All Paul's efforts after holiness, after the work of the gospel, after the eventual goal of resurrection, are not a matter of his unaided effort to do something that will make God pleased with him. They all take place within the context of God's grace: King Jesus has grasped hold of him, and all that he now does is a matter of responding in love to that firm hand on the shoulder.

LOOKING TO JESUS

Hebrews 12.1–3

[1]What about us, then? We have such a great cloud of witnesses all around us! What we must do is this: we must put aside each heavy weight, and the sin which gets in the way so easily. We must run the race that lies in front of us, and we must run it patiently. [2]We must look ahead, to Jesus. He is the one who carved out the path for faith, and he's the one who brought it to completion.

He knew that there was joy spread out and waiting for him. That's why he endured the cross, making light of its shame, and has now taken his seat at the right hand of God's throne. [3]He put up with enormous opposition from sinners. Weigh up in your minds just how severe it was; then you won't find yourselves getting weary and worn out.

I went to a school that prided itself on its outdoor pursuits. Set high in the Yorkshire Dales in north-west England, it celebrated its location in several ways, the annual climax being a ten-mile cross-country race over steep, difficult ground. Often as many as eighty or a hundred boys would enter this race, with the purpose for most of us being not to win – we left that to the serious athletes – but to get round in a reasonable time, to forge on through mud and heather until we made it back to the finish in the small town where the school was situated.

The year I ran in the race I came, if I remember rightly, about thirty-fifth; respectable though undistinguished. But the thing I remember most vividly was the final stretch, the last half mile or so. I had trained for the race over the previous weeks, and had been round the actual course several times. I was quite used to the closing stages: here we were, back again, almost at the point of a rest and a bath and a hot drink. But this time it was totally different. I had known there would be spectators, of course, but I hadn't prepared myself for the hundreds of boys, parents and local people from the town who turned out to watch as we all came back, bedraggled but mostly happy, from our hour and a half of hard work. They were cheering, waving flags, clapping and shouting encouragement and congratulations. It went on and on, down the road into the town, increasing as we got to the middle, reaching an extraordinary roar as, with a friend running beside me, I rounded the final bend and came down the road to the finish. All these people! Where had they all come from? And such noise! It felt like being a real celebrity, if only for two minutes.

Several aspects of this climactic passage in Hebrews draw on the image of the Christian pilgrimage as a long-distance race, and the first is, obviously, the 'great cloud of witnesses' all around us. Those who have gone before us, from Abel and Abraham right through to the unnamed heroes and heroines noted at the end of Hebrews chapter 11, haven't simply disappeared. They are there at the finishing line, cheering us on, surrounding us with encouragement and enthusiasm, willing us to do what they did and finish the course in fine style. The difference is, of course, that in a race the runners are competing against one another, whereas in the journeying of God's people what matters most to each runner is that all the others make it safely home as well.

What must we do to run the race with efficiency and success? The writer continues the athletic imagery to suggest three things in particular.

First, we must get rid of any heavy weights that are slowing us down. Athletes sometimes train carrying heavy packs on their backs, to build up strength and energy against the time when, for the actual race, they will run without any extra weight at all. But far too many Christians try to run the race of Christian pilgrimage while carrying all kinds of heavy baggage – anxieties about trivial concerns, ambitions to use the gospel as a means of self-advancement, resentments at other people, secret greed for the bodily appetites, and so on. In particular, it's possible for sin of one sort or another to get in the way and constrict our movement; though some translations speak here of sin 'clinging closely' to us, the word properly means 'obstructing' or 'constricting'. The writer seems to have in mind the danger an athlete might face if the track isn't completely clear – if someone puts a hurdle in the way, or leaves a bench or other object across the path of the runners. That's what sin can be like when Christians tolerate it in their lives or in the community. It gets in the way, it can trip you up, it can seriously damage your chance of completing the course.

The second point is that this race, like the ten-mile run at my school, is a long haul, and you need patience. There are always some runners who really prefer a short sprint; some of them, faced with a ten-mile run, will go far too fast at the start and then be exhausted after two or three miles. Sadly, many of us will know Christians like that too: keen and eager in their early days, they run out of steam by the time they reach mature adulthood, and by the time they're in middle age or older they have either lost all energy for active Christian living or are frantically trying to recapture the zip and sparkle of a now inappropriate teenage-style faith. Give me the person, any day, who starts a bit more slowly but who is still there, patiently running the next mile and the next and the next, all those years later.

The third point is to keep your eyes, or at least your imagination (when you're too far away to see!), fixed on the finishing line and on the one who is at the centre of the cloud of witnesses, waiting there to greet you himself. Jesus ran this course before us. In fact, he pioneered the way, opened up the course and brought it to a successful completion. Our task is to follow in his steps. He has made it across the finishing line, and his encourage-ment, and the thought of his welcome and congratulations at the end, are the central motivation for us to continue in hope, faith and patience.

The rest of the passage invites us to contemplate what exactly Jesus went through on his own patient journey, and to realize that we have mostly had an easy time of it by comparison. He kept his eye on the joy that was waiting for him – the joy of doing his father's will, of bringing his saving purpose to fulfilment – and he put up with the foul torture of crucifixion, a degrading and disgusting as well as excruciating and agonizing death. Now, as a result, he is in the key position of honour at God's right hand.

Hebrews is keenly aware that the readers are in danger of being weary with all that they are facing, day after day, in terms of threats, persecution, intimidation and mockery from their contemporaries, their neighbours and perhaps their former friends. This is like the long, hard haul up a steep and muddy hill in the middle of a long-distance race. They must keep going; they must remind themselves continually of the one who blazed this trail in the first place; they must think how much worse it was for him. That way they will be kept from becoming worn out completely. As so often in the Christian life, *reminding* your-self of *truth*, not trying to conjure up feelings of this or that sort, is the way to keep going in faith and patience.

WATCH OUT FOR DANGERS!

Hebrews 12.12–17

[12]So stop letting your hands go slack, and get some energy into your sagging knees! [13]Make straight paths for your feet. If you're lame, make sure you get healed instead of being put out of joint. [14]Follow after peace with everyone, and the holiness which is necessary before you can see the Lord. [15]Take good care that nobody lacks God's grace; don't let any 'root of bitterness

spring up to cause trouble', defiling many people. [16]No one must be immoral or worldly-minded, like Esau: he sold his birthright for a single meal! [17]You know, don't you, that later on, when he wanted to inherit the blessing, he was rejected. There was no way he could change either his mind or Isaac's, even though he wept bitterly in trying to do so.

'It was a moment of madness.'

The politician stood shamefully before the press. He had been caught out soliciting for sexual favours in a notorious part of town. His character was in ruins, his reputation in tatters. He would not now get the senior job he had coveted. There was no way back. His only excuse was that for a moment he had taken leave of his senses. Treating that statement at face value (though many doubted it at the time), it seems that one night he had made a disastrously wrong decision and was now bitterly regretting it. Human character and reputation is like a tree; it takes decades to grow, but it can be cut down or burnt to a cinder in a matter of minutes.

Well, politicians do sometimes come back after public disgrace, though in my country they seldom get very far when they try. But the point of the sharp warning in this passage is that it is indeed possible to do things which bring our character crashing down in ruins and to discover that there is no way back. The classic example we are offered here is that of Esau, the older twin brother of Jacob. His story is told in Genesis 26 and 27, and we need to remind ourselves what it's about if we're to see what Hebrews is saying here.

Jacob doesn't exactly come out of the story with his hands clean, but the focus of the story is the folly of Esau. He had been out hunting in the countryside and when he came back home Jacob was cooking a meal. Esau was famished with hunger; Jacob refused to give him food unless he gave him his rights as the firstborn son, in other words, the principal share of the inheritance from their father Isaac. Esau, it seems, happily swore away his birthright in exchange for the food. Short-term relief, long-term misery.

The plot then unwinds: Jacob tricks Isaac into thinking he is Esau and giving him his rich and full blessing. Esau comes in later and begs for a blessing as well, but is refused: Isaac has made Jacob the heir of everything, and he can't go back on it. Esau weeps, but it's all to no avail. He had sworn an oath himself, and was now (albeit through trickery) made to keep it. There was no way back, no space for a change of heart, no way he could change Isaac's mind either. In Hebrews 12.17, the text literally says 'he did not find a place of repentance'. The word for 'repentance' means 'a change of mind' or 'a change of heart', and once we think into the story we see that, though this probably refers to Esau's own desire for a change of mind, it could also refer to his attempt to change what Isaac himself had thought and done.

It's impossible. I once knew of a man who had cheated his employers. Rather than make a public scandal of the matter, the employers offered him a package deal through which, if he agreed to leave at once, he would maintain his good reputation. The man refused, whereupon he was dismissed and the matter became public. Not long afterwards he tried, through influential friends, to put pressure on the employers to restore his reputation, to say by implication at least that he had done nothing wrong. Not surprisingly, the employers refused. He had made the decision. Decisions have consequences. There was no turning back. That's the kind of situation Esau was in.

What sort of situation in the church, then and now, does Hebrews imagine will be parallel to this? From the beginning of verse 15, it looks as though the writer is aware that within every church, every Christian fellowship, there may be some people, whether few or many, who are, as it were, 'passengers'. They are enjoying being where they are; they like the company of Christian people; they feel safe and secure. But they have not done business with God for themselves. They have not sought, and found, his grace, that loving mercy which goes down to the root of their very being and transforms them at the core. Nobody, says the writer, should 'lack God's grace'. Other members of the community must take care at this point, must watch out for one another and make sure that grace reaches everyone.

Because, if people continue to miss out on knowing God's love for themselves, the warning of Deuteronomy 29.18 may come true. Deuteronomy warns that, even within the people of God themselves, there may be 'a root sprouting poisonous and bitter growth'. Sometimes, from within an apparently happy church or fellowship, discontent can arise. It may take the form of doctrinal or ethical disagreement; these can be real enough, but often they can provide a smokescreen for personal agendas. The sign is always the sense of bitterness that accompanies it. Disagreement between wise, praying Christians can take place without bitterness; where that troubling and poisonous bitterness starts to make its presence felt, we should recognize what's going on. When people are outwardly part of the community, but inwardly not completely open to God's love and leading, they are capable of saying and doing things which disgrace themselves and the community. Like Esau, they can have a moment of madness which creates a new situation, and they can't go back.

The opening verses of this passage, then, urge the readers to sort themselves out, to become the sort of people spoken of in one of the great prophetic passages, Isaiah 35. 'Strengthen the weary hands,' says the prophet, 'and make firm the feeble knees!' (35.3). God is doing a new thing in your midst – read the whole of Isaiah 35 and see – and you must stand up and get on with the job. There is no room for spiritual laziness (which often includes an element of physical laziness as well). If something is going lame, don't shrug your shoulders and say, 'Oh well, I can't do anything about it.' Make sure you find healing.

In particular, follow after peace and holiness (verse 14). Peace with all people is a fine ideal; but this writer, like Paul in Romans

12.18, knows it won't always happen. You must *pursue* it, chase after it, do all in your power to accomplish it. And holiness – well, as Hebrews says, this is what's required if you're to stand in the presence of the holy God. Don't let anyone tell you otherwise. And don't lose it all to a moment of madness.

IT'S EASY TO GET LOST

2 Peter 2.1–10a

[1]There were, however, false prophets among the people, just as there will be false teachers among yourselves, who will sneak in with their destructive false teachings, even denying the master who paid the price for them. They will earn swift destruction for themselves, [2]and many will follow after their disgusting practices. The way of truth will be blasphemed because of them, [3]and in their greed they will exploit you with fake prophecies. Their condemnation has not been idle for a long time now, and their destruction has not fallen asleep.

[4]God didn't spare the angels who sinned, you see, but he threw them into the Pit, into dark caverns, handing them over to be guarded until the time of judgment. [5]Similarly, he didn't spare the ancient world, but brought a flood on the world of the ungodly and rescued Noah, a herald of righteousness, with seven others. [6]Similarly, he condemned the cities of Sodom and Gomorrah, reducing them to ashes and ruin, thus setting up an example of what would happen to the ungodly. [7]He snatched righteous Lot out of the disaster, a man who had been deeply troubled by their shameful and unprincipled behaviour. [8]That righteous man, you see, living in their midst, could see and hear day after day lawless deeds which tortured his righteous soul. [9]The Lord knows how to rescue the godly from testing, and also how to keep the unrighteous ready for the day of judgment and punishment, [10a]especially those who follow after the pollution of fleshly lust and despise authority.

'I told you it was easy to get lost.'

Our host stood on the doorstep with a wry smile on his face. We had assumed we more or less knew the way. We have a good sense of direction. We had even been there before; surely we would remember the route once we saw the landmarks? But no: we had taken at least one wrong turning, and there wasn't an obvious way to cut across country and get back on track. So we had driven round back streets in small towns, trying to find a road that would put things right, and all the time worrying they would think we weren't coming (this was in the days before mobile phones).

No harm was done, except to our pride. But the lesson is obvious. Don't just assume, because you're a cheerful sort of person and don't like to think about possible problems, that the way will be clear and simple. It very often won't be. And this applies especially in that long, twisting, complicated journey called Christian discipleship.

How we wish things weren't like this. We would like, of course, a nice straight path, a smooth and easy road, so that we could follow Jesus cheerfully and without the worry that we might at any minute take a wrong turning. But, as Jesus himself warned us, things are not like that. Even among his own followers there was one whom he once called 'satan', and another one who did eventually do the satan's work for him.

And now Peter, remembering perhaps how easily he himself had been led astray, utters a stern warning against false teachers and prophets. How we wish this sort of thing wasn't necessary! Wouldn't it be kinder, gentler, more ... well, more *Christian*, to assume that people who claim to be speaking the truth, to be teaching the Christian way, are doing so in fact? Surely we shouldn't have such suspicious minds?

Well, the same early Christians who tell us to be kind and gentle also tell us to be on our guard against being deceived. Jesus himself told us to be not only innocent as doves but also wise as serpents. It's a difficult combination. But we won't get very far in the right direction unless we work hard on both sides of our character.

Here, obviously, Peter is going for the wisdom of the serpent. There are false prophets and false teachers; the problem is that they don't wear a label round their necks giving the game away. The devastating thing about such prophets and teachers *is that they sound all too plausible.* When you listen to them, your first impression is, 'Yes: this is good; this is what we need to hear. It may not be quite what I expected, but I like the sound of it.' Sometimes, of course, that is the sign that the teaching is genuine and true. There are indeed times when what we've heard before needs to be expanded, or seen in a different light. But sometimes this is a sign that all is not well. There is such a thing as paranoia, jumping straight to accusations of wicked heresy when in fact what is on offer is freshly glimpsed truth. But there is also, alas, such a thing as deliberately shutting your eyes to things, assuming or pretending that something is all right when in fact it's all wrong. A church, or an individual Christian, that cannot tell the difference, or that assumes everything is always going to be more or less 'all right', is in deep danger.

So Peter is putting up a sign which says, 'Danger this way!' Right off the top he is offering danger-signs. False teaching will regularly 'deny the Master', saying that Jesus is only one among many teachers, or that perhaps his death didn't really 'pay the price' (verse 1). False teaching will encourage 'disgusting practices' – Peter isn't more specific at this point, but even the general warning ought to put us on the alert (verse 2). Is this teaching telling people that behaviour which most Christians have found abhorrent is all right after all? Then he warns that 'the way of truth will be blasphemed': outsiders will look at such would-be Christian teachers and find them a soft target at which to fire their blasphemous barbs. Finally (verse 3) they may use their fake prophecies as a way of boosting income. Nothing like some strange ideas to get people buying books or signing on for lecture courses. There are always plenty of people who want to be told that proper full-blooded Christian faith and life is a mistake and that there's an easier way.

Before he goes into any more detail, Peter sends his readers back to stories they might be more familiar with than we are. These stories are all drawn from the early chapters of Genesis, and they reflect subsequent Jewish traditions in which the plots, and the characters, are developed a bit further. Peter isn't simply highlighting the dangers of false teaching and behaviour, and the fact that God will bring judgment upon such things. He is more encouraging than that. He is stressing that God will rescue his people out of the mess. Judgment and mercy: those are the solid promises upon which you can rely.

The first example refers back to the famous story of the wicked angels in Genesis 6. God has kept them guarded until the day of judgment. But judgment was swifter in the second case, that of the world at the time of Noah; and also in the third case, the destruction of Sodom and Gomorrah and the rescue of Lot. In each case, we should note, the wickedness to be judged, from which God rescues people, is not so much fancy or off-beam teaching about theoretical matters, but the practices which give the game away: sin, ungodliness, and shameful and un-principled behaviour.

Again, Peter isn't very specific, but the general sense is clear. When teachers emerge who remove the normal restraint that Christian faith, like Judaism, had imposed on human desires, we should beware. The deadly combination at which he points in verse 10a has a sharper focus: 'those who follow after the pollution of fleshly lust and despise authority'. It would be a bold person who claimed that no such problems existed in today's church. It is easy to get on the wrong road – easier than you might think.

The underlying point, though, is the positive one, and Peter states it clearly in verse 9. You are not left to your own devices. Yes, you will be tested, and yes, wicked and unscrupulous people will appear to flourish. But God is not mocked. He knows how to rescue his people from the test. And he knows how to keep the wicked ready for the day of judgment. God's judgment and mercy are, if you like, the twin characteristics which correspond to the command that we should be wise as serpents and innocent as doves. Life would be very pleasant if it was all mercy and innocence. But it isn't. It's easy to get lost.

5

THE RENEWAL OF THE WORLD

THE FIRST AND THE LAST
Matthew 19.23–30

[23]Jesus said to his disciples, 'I'm telling you the truth: it's very hard for a rich person to get into the kingdom of heaven. [24]Let me say it again: it's easier for a camel to go through the eye of a needle than for a rich person to enter God's kingdom.'

[25]The disciples were completely flabbergasted when they heard that. 'So who then can be saved?' they asked.

[26]Jesus looked round at them. 'Humanly speaking,' he replied, 'it's impossible. But everything's possible with God.'

[27]Then Peter spoke up. 'Look here,' he said, 'we've left everything behind and followed you. What can we expect?'

[28]'I'm telling you the truth,' Jesus replied. 'In God's great new world, when the son of man sits on his glorious throne, those of you who have followed me will sit on twelve thrones – yes, you! – and rule over the twelve tribes of Israel. [29]And anyone who's left houses or brothers or sisters or father or mother or children or estates because of my name will get back a hundred times over, and will inherit the life of that new age. [30]But many at the front will find themselves at the back, and the back ones at the front.'

Once, as a boy, I watched a large party of hunters on horseback chasing a fox over open country. Even if you disapprove of foxhunting, as many do, it was a fine sight on a cold wintry day. Down the hillside they came: in the front were the leaders, in red hunting uniform, on splendid horses. They were blowing horns, close behind the hounds, looking like what they were – the local gentry, landowners, the rich and well known. Behind them were other fine riders on good-quality horses, wearing brown and black hunting clothes. Behind them again, less orderly, on various types and sizes of horse, and without any real uniform except their ordinary country clothes, came a raggle-taggle group of riders, enjoying themselves but not such a fine sight.

But then, with typical cunning, the fox they were all pursuing hid in a thicket, and doubled back up the next field so that it suddenly reappeared near the top of the hill it had come from in the first place. One of the riders near the back of the pack spotted it, and blew a horn. And the whole company of riders had to turn round and go back the way they'd come.

That was the sight I remember. Leading the way, this time, were the raggle-taggle group of riders on whichever old horses they had managed to find. In the middle were the riders in brown and black. And right at the back, having got to the bottom of the long hill only to find they must turn round and go back, were the red-coated brigade, looking decidedly out of sorts and embarrassed at bringing up the rear, something they weren't used to doing either in hunting or in society.

Those at the back, said Jesus, will find themselves at the front, and those at the front will find themselves at the back. There will be astonishment, embarrassment, delight and dismay. God is going to stand everything on its head. In the long human hunt for truth, wisdom, justice and salvation, the divine fox has doubled back, and is reappearing where we least expected him. This time, the nobodies are in the lead, and the great and good are in the rear.

That is Jesus' verdict on the sorry episode of the rich young man, which the disciples then discuss with him. We should notice how amazed they were to be told that rich people would have difficulty getting into God's kingdom. They had taken it for granted that, if God had made his kingdom so that Israel, in particular, could inherit it, those who were rich and famous in Israel would certainly be guaranteed a place.

In our world, television and magazines can make people 'celebrities' on very slender grounds. People often regard rock stars, fashion icons, movie actors and sports heroes with an awe they used to reserve for royalty, or even for God. The results are plain to see, when such people turn out to have very ordinary human lives and emotions which can't take the strain that fame produces. In Jesus' world, many regarded God's promises of blessing in the Old Testament as meaning that those who seemed to have the greatest blessings in the present – in other words, the rich, titled and landed – must be God's favourites. It came as a great shock to be told otherwise. They were among the people 'at the front', who would probably end up 'at the back'.

Some people have suggested that the saying about the camel going through the eye of a needle is actually a reference to a gate in Jerusalem that was called 'the needle's eye'. A camel would need to have all it was carrying on its back unloaded to get through it. Other people have pointed out that a word very similar to 'camel' meant a sort of rope; maybe he was talking of threading a sailor's rope through a seamstress's needle. But both of these suggestions miss the point. It's like saying, 'You couldn't get a Rolls-Royce into a matchbox.' The point is not that you might achieve it if you tried very hard, or that there was a particular type of small garage called a 'matchbox'; the point is precisely that it's unthinkable. That's the moment when all human calculations and possibilities stop, and God's new possibilities start. What is impossible in human terms, Jesus' followers are to discover to their amazement, is possible to God (verse 26).

Jesus is then offering a vision of God's whole new world in which everything will be upside down and inside out. He uses pictures we have become accustomed to in the gospel story. The son of man sitting on his glorious throne takes us to chapter 7 of the prophetic book of Daniel, where God's kingdom will be established at last with the overthrow of evil and the vindication of God's people. Then those who have given up everything to follow Jesus will find themselves not only rescued from eternal death, but actually ruling with Jesus himself in the new world.

CREATION RENEWED

Romans 8.18–25

[18]This is how I work it out. The sufferings we go through in the present time are not worth putting in the scale alongside the glory that is going to be unveiled for us. [19]Yes: creation itself is on tiptoe with expectation, eagerly awaiting the moment when God's children will be revealed. [20]Creation, you see, was subjected to pointless futility, not of its own volition, but because of the one who placed it in this subjection, in the hope [21]that creation itself would be freed from its slavery to decay, to enjoy the freedom that comes when God's children are glorified.

[22]Let me explain. We know that the entire creation is groaning together, and going through labour pains together, up until the present time. [23]Not only so: we too, we who have the first fruits of the spirit's life within us, are groaning within ourselves, as we eagerly await our adoption, the redemption of our body. [24]We were saved, you see, in hope. But hope isn't hope if you can see it! Who hopes for what they can see? [25]But if we hope for what we don't see, we wait for it eagerly – but also patiently.

I walked through the wood several times before I realized what the signpost meant.

The wood was thick, with paths leading this way and that. I knew some of them quite well, and had my favourites among them. There was the one that led round by the lake, another that took you to a splendid little clearing where you would usually see rabbits and squirrels. There was another one that led past some ancient oak trees, of the sort that I imagine would have witnessed battles hundreds of years ago.

But there was another path which I had never taken. It looked a bit overgrown and I couldn't see where it would go. Because on most of my walks I'm in a hurry to get exercise and then get back to work, I never bothered with it. Nor did I give a second thought to a small post which stood, almost hidden behind bushes, just beside the start of the path. It had what looked like the letter V at the top, a foot or two from the ground. For all I knew, it was just a mark cut in the wood. It didn't necessarily mean anything.

Until one day I came past the place, and someone had cleared the bushes enough to reveal three other letters, and an arrow pointing along the path. The other letters, downwards from the V, were I, E and W. A *view*? What sort of a view? Intrigued, I took the path for the first time.

To begin with, it was as I'd expected: overgrown (I obviously wasn't the only one who'd ignored it), with brambles and thorns in the way. It was muddy underfoot, as well; I wished I'd had my thicker boots on. But then it turned sharply through the trees and began to climb quite steeply. I was out of breath in a few minutes, but after a brief pause I kept going, getting more excited. Suddenly, instead of thick trees all around me, I saw clear sky emerging. Then I was out of the trees and onto a slab of rock. I scrambled up it and stood there calling myself names for never finding the spot before.

It was indeed a view. I was looking down not only on the whole large wood but also on the little town beyond it. I could see other hills in the distance, and smoke rising from villages in between. Half the county seemed to lie there before me. And I might never have known.

Romans 8.18–25 is like that view. From this point we can see, in astonishing clarity, the whole plan of salvation for all of God's creation. Once you've glimpsed this view, you will never forget it. And yet most readers of Romans, for many years and in many traditions, have hurried on by. They have been busy with theories of individual justification and salvation. They have been eager for moral lessons, for a fresh experience of the spirit (or a fresh theology to back up the experience they've had). They have been on their way to the great questions about Israel and the Gentiles, which do indeed preoccupy a good deal of Romans.

And the signpost which might have told them to turn this way and walk up this path has been covered in bushes and brambles. The language of creation on tiptoe with expectation is not what they expect. The strange idea of God subjecting creation to futility and slavery, and of creation then being rescued, simply isn't what people wanted to hear, or knew how to interpret when they did. The old King James translation probably didn't help either, by saying 'creature' when today's word would be 'creation', giving the average reader the puzzle of wondering which 'creature' Paul was talking about. So the path to the viewpoint has been covered over with thorns and thistles. 'Strange apocalyptic ideas,' people have said, and hurried on to safer ground. But this is the place to visit. From the top of this hill you can see for ever.

Paul begins where the previous paragraph left off, with the promise that the present suffering, though often intense, will be far outweighed by 'the glory that is going to be unveiled for us'. Note, unveiled *for us*. Not 'in us', as though glorification were after all simply us looking pleased with ourselves. Not 'to us', as though we were going to be spectators of 'glory', like people watching a fireworks display. The point of 'glory' is that it means glorious, sovereign rule, sharing the Messiah's saving rule over the whole world. And that is what the whole creation is waiting for. It is waiting for us, for you and me, for all God's children, to be revealed. Then, at last, creation will see its true rulers, and will know that the time has come for it to be rescued from corruption.

To understand this, we need to grasp the big biblical story of creation. When we look at the world of creation as it is in the present, we see a world in the same condition as the children of Israel were in when they were enslaved in Egypt. Just as God allowed the Israelites to go down into Egypt, so that in bringing them out he could define them for ever as the freedom-from-slavery people, so God has allowed creation to be subjected to its present round of summer and winter, growth and decay, birth and death. It's beautiful, yes, but it always ends in tears or at least a shrug of the shoulders. If you happen to live at the sharp end of the corruption of creation – on an earthquake fault line, for instance, or by an active volcano – you may sense the awe of that futile power. Creation can sometimes appear like a caged buffalo: all that energy, and it's not achieving anything. And, thinking of wild animals, what about that promise of the wolf and the lamb lying down together? Is that just a dream?

No, says Paul, it isn't a dream. It's a promise. All these things are signs that the world as it is, though still God's good creation, and pregnant with his power and glory (1.20), is not at present the way it should be. God's 'covenant faithfulness' was always about his commitment that, through the promises to Abraham, he would one day put the whole world to rights. Now at last we see what this meant. The human race was put in charge of creation (as so often, Paul has Genesis 1—3 not far from his mind). When humans rebelled and worshipped parts of creation instead of God himself (Romans 1.21–23), creation fell into disrepair. God allowed this state of slavery to continue, not because the creation wanted to be like that but because he was determined eventually to put the world back to rights according to the original plan (just as, when Israel let him down, he didn't change the plan, but sent at last a faithful Israelite). The plan had called for human beings to take their place under God and over the world, worshipping the creator and exercising glorious stewardship over the world.

The creation isn't waiting to *share* the freedom of God's children, as some translations imply. It is waiting to benefit wonderfully when God's children are glorified. It is waiting – on tiptoe with expectation, in fact – for the particular freedom it will enjoy when God gives to his children that glory, that wise rule and stewardship, which was always intended for those who bear God's glorious image.

This perspective on the whole created order has all kinds of implications, from the way we think about the ultimate future for the world and ourselves (the end of the story is not a disembodied 'heaven' but a whole new world) to our present anticipation of that final responsibility for God's world. This is a positive, world-affirming view, without any of the risks associated with pantheism (idolatry, and the lack of any critique of evil). There are many avenues here we might like to explore.

But Paul moves at once to consider the present position of God's children in the light of this future. We are, he says, longing for the time when we ourselves will be fully and finally redeemed, when, that is, we will receive our promised resurrection bodies. We groan and sigh, if we know what we are about, as we experience the tension between the glorious promise and the present reality. This tension is encapsulated in the fact that the spirit is already at work within us, but has not yet completed the task of our full renewal. We have the 'first fruits' of the spirit's life; Paul uses the harvesting image of early sheaves offered to God as the sign of a great crop still to come. We are left with a striking analysis of Christian hope, hope that, like faith, is not seen (or it wouldn't be hope at all), but hope that is certain none the less. Groaning and waiting, eager but patient: that is the characteristic Christian stance.

Paul's larger picture locates this groaning on the map of all creation. At the centre of this remarkable passage is one of his most vivid images of hope: that of birth-pangs. The whole creation is in labour, longing for God's new world to be born. The church is called to share that pain and that hope. The church is not to be apart from the pain of the world; it is to be in prayer at precisely the place where the world is in pain. That is part of our calling, our high but strange role within God's purposes for new creation.

THE MYSTERY AND THE VICTORY

1 Corinthians 15.50–58

[50]This is what I'm saying, my dear family. Flesh and blood can't inherit God's kingdom; decay can't inherit undecaying life. [51]Look! I'm telling you a mystery. We won't all sleep; we're all going to be changed – [52]in a flash, at the blink of an eye, at the last trumpet. This is how it will be, you see: the trumpet's going to sound, the dead will be raised undecaying, and we're going to be changed. [53]This decaying body must put on the undecaying one; this dying body must put on deathlessness. [54]When the decaying puts on the undecaying, and the dying puts on the undying, then the saying that has been written will come true:

Death is swallowed up in victory!
[55]Death, where's your victory gone?
Death, where's your sting gone?

[56]The 'sting' of death is sin, and the power of sin is the law. [57]But thank God! He gives us the victory, through our Lord Jesus the Messiah.

[58]So, my dear family, be firmly fixed, unshakeable, always full to overflowing with the Lord's work. In the Lord, as you know, the work you're doing will not be worthless.

He stood there in baggy jeans, trainers, and an old sweater. 'You can't come in like that,' I said. 'This is a smart lunch, and we're the guests. We've got to get it right.'

'No problem,' he replied, and within three minutes had changed, as though miraculously, into a dark suit, a smart tie, and polished black shoes. The transformation seemed almost instantaneous.

Of course, social convention doesn't have much to do with the kingdom of God. But that's not the point. This passage is all about the instant transformation which will change, not just the outward appearance, but the inner reality of who and what we are.

Paul is here talking about the people – he assumes he will be one of them – who are still alive at the great moment when heaven is unveiled, the royal Lord reappears, the dead are raised to their new bodies, and (as he says in Romans 8) the whole creation is liberated from decay to share the freedom of the glory of God's children. There is one apparent problem remaining: what happens to those who are still alive?

In 1 Thessalonians 4.17 Paul uses picture-language of one sort, borrowed from Daniel 7: we will be caught up on the clouds to meet the Lord as he comes, so that we can then escort him royally into his kingdom, here in God's new world. But in the present passage and Philippians 3.20–21 he speaks of the same event in terms of what happens to the bodies of those concerned. The answer is simple: they will be transformed.

They need to be transformed, because the way they are at the moment is inappropriate for God's new world. It's not just like someone wearing scruffy jeans at a smart lunch; it's like somebody who is, so to speak, *made of the wrong stuff*. At the moment we are people made of corruptible, decaying material; we need to be transformed into non-corruptible, undecaying material, so that we become people over whom death has no more control.

People get puzzled when Paul says, 'Flesh and blood can't inherit God's kingdom.' Hasn't he just insisted on the bodily resurrection? And isn't 'flesh and blood' a way of saying 'body'? Does he, they wonder, mean after all that the new existence will be 'non-bodily', merely 'spiritual'?

No. When Paul uses the word 'flesh', he regularly means that there's something wrong with the material in question. Either it's in rebellion against God; or it is perishable, decaying; or both. What he here means by 'flesh and blood' is explained immediately afterwards. The present 'flesh and blood' will decay and die, but God intends to create a world – and, in Jesus, he has decisively inaugurated the project – in which decay and death are not accommodated but defeated.

The point then is that 'we shall not all sleep' – in other words, not all Christians will die before the great day – but 'we shall all be changed'. We shall be transformed. It will happen in a flash, in a great act of new creation, echoing round the cosmos like the blast of a great trumpet. When this happens, the ancient story which the Bible told in a thousand different ways will come true: the story of creation reaching its intended goal; the story of the enemies being defeated (Egypt, Assyria, Babylon, Syria and many others – and now the ultimate ones, sin and death); the story of God's victory, the creator's victory, over all the forces of chaos and destruction.

Paul here quotes from two biblical passages, Isaiah 25 and Hosea 13, which pointed in this direction. But this truth, like that of Jesus' own death and resurrection, is not simply established through one or two proof-texts. It is in line with the entire narrative. Death has claimed a victory, and the pagan world shrugs its shoulders and acknowledges it. The Jewish world at its best declares that God remains the creator and will do a new thing. The Christian message is that he *has already done the new thing* in the Messiah, Jesus, and that he *will* do it for all Jesus' people through the power of the spirit. And in that new thing death and decay will be gone, swallowed up for ever.

Paul pauses to glance sideways at the ways in which death has worked. It gets its peculiar character, its unpleasant 'sting', through sin, the dark power that entices humans to rebellion, to turn away from God the life-giver. And sin gets its particular power, in Paul's world, from the law. Paul doesn't explain what he means here, and we need Romans 7.1—8.11 to get inside this cryptic throwaway line. But his main point is clear: through our Lord Jesus, the Messiah, God *has* given us the victory over all the powers that drag us down, he *will* give it to us in the future, and he *is* giving it to us here and now.

The 'here and now' is where Paul ends up. You might think, after a spectacular chapter like this one, that he would conclude by saying something like, 'So let's rejoice at the wonderful hope we can look forward to!' But he doesn't. And this isn't just because he is a solid and sober practical theologian, true though that is. It's because the truth he has been expounding, the truth of the resurrection of the dead and the transformation of the living, is not just a truth about the future hope. It's a truth about the present significance of what we are and do. *If it is true that God is going to transform this present world, and renew our whole selves, bodies included, then what we do in the present time with our bodies, and with our world, matters.* For far too long many Christians have been content to separate out future hope from present responsibility, but that is precisely what Paul refuses to do. His full-bodied doctrine and promise of resurrection sends us back to our present world, and our present life of bodily obedience to our Lord, in the glorious but sobering knowledge that, if there is continuity between who and what we are in the present and who and what we will be in the future, we cannot discount the present life, the present body and the present world as irrelevant.

On the contrary. It is a matter of the greatest encouragement to Christian workers, most of whom are away from the public eye, unsung heroes and heroines, getting on faithfully and quietly with their God-given tasks, that what they do 'in the Lord' during the present time will last, will matter, will stand for all time. *How* God will take our prayer, our art, our love, our writing, our political action, our music, our honesty, our daily work, our pastoral care, our teaching, our whole selves – how God will take this and weave its varied strands into the glorious tapestry of his new creation, we can at present have no idea. *That* he will do so is part of the truth of the resurrection, and perhaps one of the most comforting parts of all.

WISDOM FOR THE RULERS
Ephesians 3.8–13

[8]I am the very least of all God's people. However, he gave me this task as a gift: that I should be the one to tell the Gentiles the good news of the king's wealth, wealth no one could begin to count. [9]My job is to make clear to everyone just what the secret plan is, the purpose that's been hidden from the very beginning of the world in God who created all things. [10]This is it: that God's wisdom, in all its rich variety, was to be be made known to the rulers and authorities in the heavenly places – through the church!

[11]This was God's eternal purpose, and he's accomplished it in King Jesus our Lord. [12]We have confidence, and access to God, in him, in full assurance, through his faithfulness. [13]So, I beg you: don't lose heart because of my sufferings on your behalf! That's your glory!

There was once a young prince whose distant uncle was king of a great empire. The prince was carefree and happy, neither very rich nor very poor. One day, a great disaster struck. The king, his uncle, was killed in an earthquake, and all the senior members of the royal family died with him. The prince was solemnly informed that he, now, was to be king.

The prince remembered the stories he had heard of young kings in days gone by. He knew at once what he needed: wisdom. Like King Solomon, David's son and heir, he needed to know instinctively the best way of resolving a difficult situation. He needed to be able to see to the heart of the deepest and most subtle issues. The big picture and the little details; the well-pondered great questions, and the sharp, incisive practical judgment. That's what wisdom was all about, and he determined to seek it and make it his own.

There is a book called 'The Wisdom of Solomon', probably written about the time of Jesus. It's in the 'apocrypha' (Jewish books which were valued by Jews of the time, and by the early church, but not considered part of the Old Testament). One of the main themes of this book is a message to pagan rulers: what you need is wisdom! And the place to get this wisdom, according to the book, is in respecting the one true God and the people who honour him – in other words, Israel's God, and the true Israelites.

This can, of course, be turned around as a message to Israel itself. Your task, this message says, is to worship and honour the living God, whatever the pagan nations may do to you. Eventually they will realize that true wisdom consists in respecting and honouring this God, and you are to be the sign to them that this is so.

There are several passages in Paul's writings where he seems to show knowledge of 'The Wisdom of Solomon', and this is one of them. The heart of the present passage is verse 10, which is one of the New Testament's most powerful statements of the reason for the church's existence: the rulers and authorities must be confronted with God's wisdom, in all its rich variety, and this is to happen through the church! Not, we should quickly add, through what the church *says*, though that is vital as well. Rather, through what the church *is*, namely, the community in which men, women and children of every race, colour, social and cultural background come together in glad worship of the one true God.

It is precisely this many-sided, many-coloured, many-splendoured identity of the church that makes the point. God's wisdom, Paul is saying, is like that too: like a many-faceted diamond which twinkles and sparkles with all the colours in the rainbow. The 'rulers and authorities', however – both the earthly authorities and their shadowy heavenly counterparts – always tend to create societies and social structures in their own flat, boring image, monochrome, uniform and one-dimensional. Worse: they tend to marginalize or kill people or groups who don't fit their narrow band of acceptability. The church is to be, by the very fact of its existence, a warning to them that their time is up, and an announcement to the world that there is a different way to be human.

GODLINESS AND CONTENTMENT

1 Timothy 6.6–10

⁶If it's gain you want, though, there is plenty to be had in godliness – if it's combined with contentment. ⁷We brought nothing into the world, after all, and we certainly can't take anything out. ⁸If we have food and clothing, we should be satisfied with it. ⁹People who want to be rich, by contrast, fall into temptation and a trap, and many foolish and dangerous lusts which drown people in devastation and destruction. ¹⁰The love of money, you see, is the root of all evil. Some people have been so eager to get rich that they have wandered away from the faith and have impaled themselves painfully in several ways.

It is hardly an exaggeration to say that this famous passage is an indictment of modern Western culture. Never before in history has there been such a restless pursuit of riches, by more and more highly developed means. Never before has the love of money been elevated to the highest and greatest good, so that if someone asks you, 'Why did you do that?' and you responded, 'Because I could make more money that way', that would be the end of the conversation. Never before have so many people tripped over one another in their eagerness to get rich and thereby impaled themselves on the consequences of their own greed.

The greatest irony of it all is that it's done in the name of contentment – or, which is more or less the same thing, happiness. Many people give lip-service to the maxim that 'money can't buy you happiness', but most give life-service to the hope that it just might, after all. 'The pursuit of happiness', and the idea that this is a basic human right, is all very well, but when it's taken to mean the unfettered pursuit of wealth it turns into a basic human wrong. And yet every advertisement, every other television programme, many movies and most political manifestos are designed, by subtle and not-so-subtle ways, to make us say, 'If only I had just a bit more money, then I would be content.' Nelson Rockefeller, one of the richest men of his day, is reputed to have summed it up. When asked by a reporter how much money he reckoned he needed to live on comfortably, he replied, 'A little more than I get.' Most of us, from the quite poor to the very rich, would be tempted to say 'Amen' to that.

We all know the counter-argument, though it doesn't do much (granted the continual cultural bombardment) for our mental stability on the subject. If you make a lot of money, you might want to buy more houses and more wonderful things to put in them; whereupon you multiply the risk of burglary, so you get more expensive burglar alarms and insurance policies, and you end up employing people to look after you and your property. So you need to make more money again, and for that you will need to hire accountants, and probably lawyers too, not to mention investment advisors and stockbrokers. And meanwhile the monkey on your shoulder is whispering that maybe you should try this scheme to get a bit richer ... and then this one ... and now what about this ... If only you had a bit more, you could relax and be content. But in fact the only way to contentment is to sack the monkey and be content with what you have.

Of course, there are plenty of people in the world who live on or below the actual poverty line. For them, earning a little more really would make the difference between sheer misery and at least the chance of contentment. But, usually, they don't suffer much from the love of money. They are not staying up half the night devising more and more complicated ways of multiplying their wealth. Getting a job, or a slightly better job, will do the trick. Then the real things in life – food, family, house, clothes – will follow.

This paragraph is full of solid (though to us difficult) wisdom. The point is that the present world, the created order in which we live, is full of all kinds of good things. We should enjoy them in their appropriate ways, and, by thanking God for them, maintain the careful balance of neither worshipping the created world nor imagining that it's evil. But when money comes into the equation everything looks different. Money is not, as it stands, God's creation, but a human invention to make the exchange of goods easier and more flexible. The further it becomes removed from the goods themselves, and the more it becomes a 'good' in itself, the closer we come to idolatry. A society which values wealth for its own sake – which is where the Western world has been for at least the last few decades – has forgotten something vital about being human. Money itself isn't evil; but, as verse 10 famously puts it, loving money is not only evil, it's the root of all evils.

People sometimes challenge that analysis. The rapist doesn't attack out of love for money. The sadistic torturer wants to cause pain and would actually pay for the privilege of doing so. But even with sex and power, money isn't far away. Many rapists have had their appetites titillated by a culture which has soaked us in sex in order to get us to part with our money. Many who have fallen in love with firearms, weapons, and all the accoutrements of a life of violence, have gone that way because someone was eager to make money out of them. And, at the international scale, we can see only too easily how it works. Industrial giants give huge donations to a political party. When the party gets into power, it awards its friends huge contracts. Often these include, or even focus upon, the manufacture of arms. Why do we need arms? Why, to fight a war, of course. And so we go looking for one, not primarily to do justice in the world but to feed the monkey on the shoulder. And this time we impale not only ourselves, but also many others, on the bayonets and lances of our own greed.

It's a sorry picture. But in the background stands Paul saying *'There is a different way'*. We don't have to live like that. What's more, the church is called to model the different way. Do we have the courage to try?

GOD'S PATIENCE

2 Peter 3.11–18

[11]Since everything is going to dissolve in this way, what sort of people should you be? You should live lives that are holy and godly, [12]as you look for God's day to appear, and indeed hurry it on its way – the day because of which the heavens will be set on fire and dissolved, and the elements will melt with heat. [13]But we are waiting for new heavens and a new earth, in which justice will be at home. That is what he has promised.

[14]So, my dear family, as you wait for these things, be eager to be found without spot or blemish before him, in peace. [15]And when our Lord waits patiently to act, see that for what it is – salvation! Our beloved brother Paul has written to you about all this, according to the wisdom that has

been given him, [16]speaking about these things as he does in all his letters. There are some things in them which are difficult to understand. Untaught and unstable people twist his words to their own destruction, as they do with the other scriptures.

[17]But as for you, my dear family, be on your guard, since you have been warned in advance. That way you won't be led astray through the error of lawless people and fall away from your own solid grounding. [18]Instead, grow in grace and in the knowledge of our Lord and saviour Jesus the Messiah. To him be glory both now and in the day when God's new age dawns. Amen.

By the time 2 Peter was written, Paul's letters had already been circulating for some while in many of the churches, both in Turkey and Greece (where all of Paul's letters except Romans were addressed), and possibly further afield as well. Many early Christians were energetic travellers, and there is every indication that texts – letters, gospels and so on – were copied, taken from place to place, and studied. And what Peter is saying here fits closely with a theme which, though not all readers of Paul now realize it, is in fact very important in his writings as well. Peter has already spoken in this chapter of the patience to which we are called: patience in our dealings with one another, patience with God as we wait for the day of the Lord (2 Peter 3.8–9). Now we must consider God's own patience.

This is, after all, the right way round. We might present a somewhat comical sight, stamping our little feet with impatience while the creator and ruler of the universe calmly goes about his own business, knowing infinitely more than we do about how to run his world. No: the proper perspective is to regard anything that looks to us like 'delay' as an indication not that we have to be patient with God, but that God is having to be patient with us.

Which is just as well. If God were to foreclose on the world, and on ourselves, straight away, what would happen? This was already a theme which Jews before the time of Jesus were pondering, as they agonized over the apparently endless delay in waiting for God's promises to be fulfilled. God, they concluded, was holding back the great day, leaving a space for more people to repent, for lives to be transformed, for the world to come to its senses. One should be grateful for this 'patience', not angry with God for failing to hurry up when we wanted him to.

This is very much what Paul has in mind in a passage like Romans 2.1–11. It might be worth looking that up and pondering it; perhaps this is the sort of passage Peter has in mind. For Paul, 'God's kindness is meant to bring you to repentance' (Romans 2.4). But if you don't avail yourself of that opportunity, the result will be the opposite: what you do instead with that time, with that interval before final judgment, will just make matters worse when the day finally arrives (Romans 2.5–11).

This seems to be what Peter is saying, too. 'When our Lord waits patiently to act, see that for what it is – salvation!' (verse 15). God's patience is our opportunity. It is our chance to work on the holy, godly lives we ought to be living. It is our chance, too, to spread the gospel in the world. Since we know that the day is coming, the day when new heavens and new earth will emerge, filled to the brim with God's wonderful justice, his glorious setting-right of all things, we should be working towards that already, here and now.

This is the point where a wrong view of what God intends to do will really damage both our understanding and our behaviour. If we imagine that God wants simply to burn up the present world entirely, leaving us as disembodied souls in some kind of timeless 'eternity', then why should we worry about what we do here and now? What does it matter? Why not just enjoy life as best we can and wait for whatever is coming next – which is of course the answer that many philosophies have given, in the first century as well as today.

But if God intends to *renew* the heavens and the earth – as Isaiah had promised all those years before (Isaiah 65.17; 66.22), then what we do in the present time matters. It matters for us that we are 'without spot or blemish' (verse 14). It matters for God's world as a whole.

QUESTIONS FOR DISCUSSION
AND REFLECTION

1 THE WISDOM OF THE SPIRIT

God's powerful mystery (1 Corinthians 2.1–5)

How and why do the deepest mysteries of human life – such as love, death, joy and beauty – point to the mystery of God?

God's strange wisdom (1 Corinthians 2.6–13)

Why did the rulers of Jesus' time fail to understand who Jesus was?

Spiritual or merely human? (1 Corinthians 2.14—3.4)

In what respects do you feel in special need of 'the mind of the Messiah'?

Everything belongs to you (1 Corinthians 3.18–23)

When have you needed to reject the wisdom of the world in order to be open to God's wisdom?

The challenge of faith (James 1.2–8)

According to James, wisdom is needed to cope with trials and develop patience. Why does he emphasize asking for wisdom with faith?

True and false wisdom (James 3.13–18)

How do you tell the difference between God's wisdom – the 'wisdom from above' – and earthly wisdom?

2 THE TRANSFORMATION OF THE SELF

The living sacrifice (Romans 12.1–2)

Why do you think Paul emphasizes the need for the renewal of your mind?

Fruit of the spirit (Galatians 5.22–26)

In what ways could you do more to cultivate and express the fruit of the spirit?

Off with the old, on with the new (Ephesians 4.17–24)

When it comes to changing your way of life, would you say the mind is the place to start or the body? Why?

Joy and peace in God (Philippians 4.2–9)

Can you think of instances where conflict between Christians has been dealt with in a positive and healing manner?

Dying and rising with Christ (Colossians 2.20—3.4)

Have you ever felt attracted to forms of 'quick-fix' spirituality? What is it about genuinely Christian spirituality that makes it different, and in the end the wiser choice?

The new way of life (1 Peter 3.8–16)

What attitudes do Christians need to adopt when faced with (unfair) criticism or rejection because of their faith, or even just for doing good?

Building a Christian character (2 Peter 1.1–11)

Why do you need to 'run away from the corruption of lust' before you can build a Christian character?

3 THE GREATEST OF THE VIRTUES

The most important commandment (Mark 12.28–34)

Can you think of instances in your life or in the life of your church when the spiritual priorities expressed by Jesus here have been forgotten? What happened as a result?

Love one another (John 15.9–17)

In what practical ways can you love others in the same way that Jesus loves you?

The character of love (1 Corinthians 13.1–7)

Are there any aspects of Paul's description of love that you have neglected and allowed to languish? If so, what steps could you take to nurture and develop them?

God is love (1 John 4.7–21)

What connection does John make between human love and God's love? And why is it that the love he describes leaves no room for fear?

4 THE PATH OF THE DISCIPLE

Do not worry (Matthew 6.25–34)

What one thing can you do this week to start practising the wisdom of living in the present, and setting your heart on God's priorities?

The wise and wicked slaves (Matthew 24.45–51)

Think of times when you have forgotten to 'keep watch' on your actions and neglected to behave in the way God expects of you. How can you improve your efforts to prevent this happening again?

The wise and foolish girls (Matthew 25.1–13)

What in your life commonly distracts or hinders you from being ready and alert to your responsibilities as a disciple?

Where two roads lead (Romans 6.20–23)

Think about examples of constructive or destructive behaviour that you have heard of recently. How has that behaviour tended towards life or death for those involved?

Chasing on to the finish (Philippians 3.12–16)

How has God helped you to gain greater wisdom and spiritual maturity through difficult experiences in your life?

Looking to Jesus (Hebrews 12.1–3)

Are there times when you feel drained and wearied by the demands of Christian discipleship? What three things does this passage advise you to do in order to keep going?

Watch out for dangers! (Hebrews 12.12–17)

What, in your experience, are the most common factors that can make a 'root of bitterness spring up to cause trouble' among Christians? What steps can you and your fellow disciples take to prevent this happening among you?

It's easy to get lost (2 Peter 2.1–10a)

In what situations might you need to be 'wise as serpents and innocent as doves'? And how might that help you to discern between true and false teachers?

5 THE RENEWAL OF THE WORLD

The first and the last (Matthew 19.23–30)

Why does God's new world come about through the reversal of human ideas of kingship, power and greatness?

Creation renewed (Romans 8.18–25)

Given God's plan for the renewal of creation, what are the implications for the way Christians view and treat that creation now – both as individuals and as a society?

The mystery and the victory (1 Corinthians 15.50–58)

Are there times when you feel that the work you do 'in the Lord' is too small to make a difference? How does this passage encourage you in those times?

Wisdom for the rulers (Ephesians 3.8–13)

How does your church confront the world's rulers and authorities with God's wisdom? In what ways, and in what circumstances, should this happen?

Godliness and contentment (1 Timothy 6.6–10)

In what ways does the love of money act as a catalyst for evil in the present world? How can you and other Christians effectively warn and witness against this?

God's patience (2 Peter 3.11–18)

Knowing that God intends to renew the heavens and the earth, how should this affect what you do with your life in the meantime?